Opportunity Knocks: USING PR

Laurie Mercer and Jennifer Singer

Chilton Book Company
Radnor, Pennsylvania

Copyright © 1989 by Laurie Mercer and Jennifer Singer
All Rights Reserved
Published in Radnor, Pennsylvania 19089, by Chilton Book Company

No part of this book may be reproduced, transmitted, or stored
in any form or by any means, electronic or mechanical,
without prior written permission from the publisher.

Designed by Arlene Putterman
Manufactured in the United States of America

Library of Congress Cataloging in Publication Data

Mercer, Laurie.
    Opportunity knocks : using PR / Laurie Mercer and Jennifer Singer.
        p.   cm.
    Includes index.
    ISBN 0–8019–7884–x
    1. Public relations.   I. Singer, Jennifer.   II. Title.
HD59.M39   1989
659.2—dc19   88-43402
                                                            CIP

1 2 3 4 5 6 7 8 9 0   8 7 6 5 4 3 2 1 0 9

Opportunity Knocks

*To Jack and Eddy Mercer
and Fred and Leslie Glassberg*

Contents

x | Contents

Acknowledgments

The authors wish to thank the Rochester (N.Y.) Literary Center, Writers & Books, director Joe Flaherty, former assistant director Larry Champoux, and its retreat, The Gell House in Naples, New York. Also essential, in alphabetical order, were: the Atlanta Public Library, Judy Cerqua, Colleen Cottrell, Ceil Goldman, Adam and Amanda Hindson, Renee Lewis, *The New York Times* (and every other newspaper ever printed, whether fit or not), Teresa Phillips, the Public Relations Society of America, Paul Singer, and an assortment of cats.

165   PUBLIC RELATIONS MANAGEMENT OCCUPATIONS

This group includes occupations concerned with selection or development of favorable persuasive material and its distribution through personal contact or various communications media, in order to promote goodwill, develop credibility, or create favorable public image for individual, establishment, group, or organization. Includes both generalists and specialists working either as outside consultant or in-house staff member.

165.067-010   PUBLIC-RELATIONS REPRESENTATIVE (profess. & kin.)
public-relations practitioner.

Plans and conducts public relations program designed to create and maintain favorable public image for employer or client: Plans and directs development and communication of information designed to keep public informed of employer's programs, accomplishments, or point of view. Arranges for public-relations efforts in order to meet needs, objectives, and policies of individual, special interest group, business concern, nonprofit organization, or governmental agency, serving as in-house staff member or as outside consultant. Prepares and distributes fact sheets, news releases, photographs, scripts, motion pictures, or tape recordings to media representatives and other persons who may be interested in learning about or publicizing employer's activities or message. Purchases advertising space and time as required. Arranges for and conducts public-contact programs designed to meet employer's objectives, utilizing knowledge of changing attitudes and opinions of consumers, clients, employees, or other interest groups. Promotes goodwill through such publicity efforts as speeches, exhibits, films, tours, and question/answer sessions. Represents employer during community projects and at public, social, and business gatherings. May specialize in researching data, creating ideas, writing copy, laying out artwork, contacting media representatives, or representing employer directly before general public. May specialize in one type of public-relations effort, such as fund-raising campaigns or political issues. May specialize in disseminating facts and information about organization's activities or governmental agency's programs to the general public and be known as PUBLIC INFORMATION OFFICER (profess. & kin.).

From the New York State Department of Labor directory

Opportunity Knocks

The Butterfly Factor: An Introduction to Getting and Keeping Positive Attention

Many people could establish effective public relations *if* they had the information they need about how to create dynamic communications tools. That's why we wrote *Opportunity Knocks: Using PR*. We believe every person and every group should get the positive attention they deserve.

But there's more to public relations than just gaining attention. You also want to maintain that positive image. So we've told you how to write a public relations communications plan, which includes how to do research, how to handle a crisis, and how to evaluate your results. You'll learn techniques for writing press releases, approaching the media, staging a press conference, and creating a videotape press release to achieve a variety of communications goals.

Opportunity Knocks: Using PR can help you promote yourself and gain visibility for your company, profes-

1

sional organization, civic group, and political or social concern. We have tried to cover all the fundamentals and fine points of public relations know-how.

This book is like a road map. It will guide you along the way, but getting to your ultimate destination is up to you. The quality of the results you achieve will be directly related to two factors: (1) your persistence, commitment, and energy, and (2) a special attitude toward communication that will help you hear opportunity knock.

We begin with an interesting story to help illustrate that second element—attitude. Ken Wells, a reporter for the *Wall Street Journal,* profiled two companies whose California headquarters occupied a piece of ground—called a "critical habitat"—that was also home to the Bay checkerspot, a yellow, black, and orange butterfly.

Because the Bay checkerspot was about to be added to the federal endangered-species list, the green rolling hills near San Jose became a battleground between industry and environmentalists.

One of the companies, a large national defense contractor with more than 5,000 acres to share with the checkerspot, declared war on the butterfly. In public testimony, the contractor stated that to abide by the butterfly protection program could delay delivery of the Minuteman and Tomahawk missile propulsion systems.

Euphydryas editha bayensis, commonly known as the Bay checkerspot. Photo courtesy of the Stanford University Department of Biological Sciences.

The other company involved, a large waste-disposal concern, heard opportunity knocking. It responded to the tension-filled situation with some excellent public relations. While the defense contractor hired a biologist to fly a helicopter over the site, dispute the environmentalists' reports, and threaten the proposed endangered-species listing, the waste-management company protected the butterfly with a company preserve and made it the mascot of its 800-acre local landfill. In addition, the company helped improve its public image by using the butterfly in a series of well-produced television commercials.

The waste-disposal company even posted "Butterfly Crossing" signs at the plant entrance. According to one company official, "It could have been a serious problem for us, but we chose preservation as the way to go."

As the story illustrates, good public relations doesn't just happen—and, for that matter, neither does *bad* public relations. Opportunity doesn't ask permission to knock on your door. It requires a positive attitude and proven techniques to take advantage of every communications butterfly that flutters in your direction.

Telling Opportunity
Where to Knock

What is Public Relations, Anyway?

By 1990, public relations will be a $0.5-billion-a-year industry with an anticipated growth rate of 12 percent, according to a security investment research report. Of the many segments of the profession, financial public relations is expected to grow the fastest. In fact, the business horizon for public relations is actually rosier than for the far more mature disciplines of advertising and sales promotion.

It's fair to say that as a profession public relations has a relatively short history. (The phrase "public relations" wasn't uttered until 1919.) In the 1960s and 1970s, public relations became part of the national consciousness. Today, the business of public relations has never been more popular or more lucrative.

With its roots in the philosophies of P. T. Barnum, John D. Rockefeller, and Henry Ford, public relations today reflects both the early days of publicity stunts and simple image building and the present-day art of influencing top-level policy decision-making and public opinion on a global scale. Public relations gathers market research, incorporates strategic planning, and uses every motivational device possible—from press releases to elaborate satellite conferencing—to influence the media positively. Thus, when television evangelists, leaders in the field of mass communication, use satellite transmission, the effect is global (if not heaven-sent).

Most public relations projects have four elements: research, planning, execution, and evaluation. As a public relations practitioner, you have to understand each element in depth and know how it interacts with the other three. In practice, for instance, your evaluation will lead you back to research, allowing you to create a dynamic of communications activities. These elements are the basis of this book.

Six Advantages of Good PR

Economy, reach, credibility, interest, lead generation, and image enhancement are six prime advantages inherent in doing public relations.

PUBLIC RELATIONS IS ECONOMICAL. Public relations involves creating targeted communications vehicles that are meant to reach a clearly defined audience. Because the vehicles used are specially tailored for and directed to limited audiences, public relations efforts can be less expensive than advertising campaigns and yet be more effective. The rising cost of advertising space, especially television time, has contributed to the expansion of public relations as an economical, effective method to reach potential customers for a product or service.

PUBLIC RELATIONS EXTENDS REACH. Public relations enables companies and organizations to go beyond the traditional audience for advertising. For example, many hospitals today urge the parents of children who need organ transplants to "go public" with their case. These public relations campaigns, often coordinated by experienced professionals, have successfully convinced families to donate the organs of loved ones who died in the hospital and have raised thousands of dollars to cover the cost of transplant operations. They have reached far wider audiences than local appeals or advertising campaigns.

The Du Pont Company recently extended the reach of its publicity efforts by celebrating the fiftieth anniversary of nylon. The media coverage included articles in women's magazines and other outlets that the chemical company's normal advertising efforts do not reach.

PUBLIC RELATIONS ADDS CREDIBILITY. People—even public relations people—have a strong inclination to believe what they read in newspapers, magazines, and newsletters or what they see on television or listen to on the radio. When the media use the material you as a public relations practitioner provide (and we urge you to think of yourself as a professional), you are effectively creating a "third-party endorsement."

PUBLIC RELATIONS MEASURES INTEREST. Public relations involves knowing when and how to communicate with the media to get coverage of an event, cause, product, person, or even a point of view. This is achieved against long odds because many other people also are clamoring for the attention they think they or their cause deserves. The publicity you get is a sure indicator of public interest. By evaluating customer and prospect reaction to the announcement you send to the media, you become quickly aware of the product's (or person's) appeal, be it narrow or global, based on the results you achieve.

PUBLIC RELATIONS GENERATES LEADS. We live in a society that likes to be told where to go to buy something, how to volunteer or receive a service, and where and how to meet people. Public relations can create anything from an inquiry for a product or service to a starting point for a sales call.

PUBLIC RELATIONS BUILDS OR ENHANCES AN IMAGE. John D. Rockefeller hired a public relations practitioner to correct what he believed to be his poor public image.

Rockefeller had donated lots of money to charity but was presented as a skinflint by the press. By incorporating strategic public relations practices, such as working closely with newspaper reporters and creating a series of autobiographical articles, public opinion gradually shifted so that by the time Rockefeller died, a favorable image was firmly established. Few American children of the 1950s, in fact, grew up without hearing about Rockefeller's penchant for giving away dimes—a clever part of the public relations strategy.

CASE HISTORY ●

Working Smart

You are responsible for the public relations of a local arts group. You need to produce a brochure for an upcoming series of workshops. Without asking you, the arts group has already decided it wants to mail the brochure to a list of prominent arts patrons in the community. In addition to the target mailing list, the public library, other arts groups, and local theaters and art galleries have also agreed to distribute the brochure as part of the "umbrella" approach to reaching the local arts community.

Not a bad idea, but certainly not enough for a full-blown public relations effort. Knowing how to add a little extra to get results is one of the tools of the trade.

As a public relations person, you will want to write, edit, print, and mail the piece—with all materials completed—several weeks before the event. Now is the time to establish a project timeline, estimating how long each task will take and how much staff and budget will be required. (Stuffing envelopes, for instance, is just one such task.) For really large mailings (say 100 or more), you might look to an outside service. The companies who will copy your press kit materials and stuff them in addressed envelopes are usually listed in the Yellow Pages under "Mailing Services" or "Fulfillment Houses."

Many nonprofit organizations don't have staff members to help with projects, much less room in the budget for hiring an outside service. But they do have volunteers, one of the most valuable tools of the public relations person involved in a community group. Volunteers often help with clerical tasks such as stuffing envelopes, running the copier, typing mailing labels, and even organizing an entire mailing. Using volunteers does several things for an organization: It enables the group to save money, enhances the group's image as one that's actively involved in the community, and creates a group of dedicated people who will spread the word about the group's value to the community. Volunteers themselves also can become a source of public relations materials. Many nonprofit organizations use stories about especially dedicated or interesting volunteers to gain media interest.

O.K., you've mailed the workshop brochure. Time to go home, right? Wrong. That's only the front end, as they say in computertalk. Now people are going to respond to the brochure and, as its creator, you have to respond to the reaction it receives. Using the "run-it-up-the-flagpole" metaphor, you need to count the people who saluted it.

Soon, your phone is ringing as people call for more information. Some workshops offering live models fill up quickly, but antique stenciling hasn't got many takers.

Several people complain that the brochure arrived just days before the first workshop, too late for them to be able to attend. You feel like telling them about the changes in production processes that held everything up for a week because the instructor for Raku pottery died while riding his lawnmower, but you decide to hold your breath. This is the service industry, after all; you get paid to be nice, and even helpful.

You want to keep track of all responses—positive, negative, and undecided. This is where the job gets easier if you have a staff to support your activities. For the short term, you have questions to answer, signs to post ("Free Parking Here for Arts Center"), and people to contact to keep the communications effort pro-active, ongoing, and strong.

A call to the arts critic on the local newspaper might get you quick coverage of the workshops that need help. Some research into what type of person did sign up might indicate a new method of promoting the workshop. The antique stenciling course had only three. Maybe no one cared about the subject. If no one signs up for the next stenciling series, recommend to the administrators that they drop the workshop. But perhaps with proper "positioning" (presentation) of the course, you as a communications professional may be able to pique interest.

For example, why not incorporate a field trip to the local country or folk art museum for that hands-on approach? Make sure the course and field trip will be accessible to the handicapped, and have an instructor who uses sign language for the hearing impaired. Or reorganize the course and materials to provide a mini-outreach class for the homebound elderly or other special populations of older citizens who might enjoy a new hobby.

Following the launch, it's time to refine the mailing list. People who enrolled for the first session are a prime audience for your next mailing. Weed out those who haven't attended openings or events for some time; they're probably not interested, and they're costing the organization money to reach. If you have any doubts about someone's interest, include a "drop dead" letter—a letter that requires a positive response to your mailing by a certain date to remain on the organization's mailing list.

This list, by the way, is part of what is known as your database. Database manipulation is the heart and soul of direct marketing (to some, also known as junk mail—you know, the envelopes with the glassine windows in them).

The key to successful direct marketing is the same as for any effective two-way communication: Listen carefully to the target audience and then respond with a product or service in a way that reflects creativity, interest, and honesty to make your public relations effort stand out. That's what it's all about—getting the positive attention you and your cause deserve.

Making Things Happen with PR

Think about it: Whoever heard of a *bad* opportunity? Public relations offers a way to create a "wish list" and then to plan a strategy that will make those wishes come to fruition, with some time, patience, and a little help from this book. In addition to cost effectiveness, public relations can give your message greater credibility than can advertising, which pays for its space.

Visualize your project, product, client, interest, or whatever you want to promote. Think: "I would like to get more visibility for my idea in print, radio, or the electronic media."

Keep many fires burning. Even if you can't have the cover of *Time*, you might get five free minutes on an early-morning talk show. Focus on what's happening and what you could do to help your projects along.

What's the easiest way to get into print? Opportunities always exist. After all, we are a news-consuming country. Try the Letters to the Editor column. They are widely read. But having something to say that is worth saying is where the sound of opportunity knocking comes in. If you have a major story, go for national publicity, but if it's a pancake breakfast, concentrate on getting visibility where it will do the most good—local papers, posters in the supermarket, and welcome signs in front of the building at least a week in advance.

And anticipate spending about three times as much time pursuing opportunities as you do developing your tools of the trade—the press releases, press kits, speeches, bylined expertise articles, audiovisual and videotape scripts, communications plans, and special-events planning that gain visibility for you or your project. It may take only an hour to write the release, but you'll spend time thinking and planning beforehand, and hours placing it and following up.

Media people change jobs more frequently than Willie Shoemaker changes horses. But a call ahead to find out who handles the wire service for UPI and AP in your town, or the name of the assignment editor, feature story writer, weekend news desk editor, sports editor, or person in charge of restaurant reviews, will help you get the attention you need for your news.

One television news director summarized the placement process with these observations: The assignment editor is key. There are 11 minutes of actual news for each 30-minute news program, and an average station in a midsize city receives about 90 requests for publicity each day, so brevity in your press release is everything. The lead time for a simple story is 10 days, while a complex one requires two weeks. Send color slides or videotapes to TV stations to increase their interest. Follow-up phone calls are essential.

As a final step, if you need to demonstrate your communications effectiveness to the people who supply the budget that enables you to do your work, get every clip you can and include the number of people who probably read or watched it. The reps who sell space and time at the station/newspaper are happy to share those statistics. Then ask for the amount of money it would take to fill six inches or the two minutes of air time you achieved and you've got your proof. You can now use all of this in a report for your client or management.

CASE HISTORY ●

Here's How It Happens

STAFF: One public relations professional, a freelance publicist, and a supervisor involved enough to ride a bicycle to accompany a blind marathon runner in the actual event.

TIME FRAME: One year prior to event.

ACTIVITY: A local company (RCI), a long-distance telephone carrier, decides to co-sponsor the city marathon. Almost immediately, the public relations person begins a series of what becomes an involved, complex round of meetings between RCI, which she represents, and the participants and the community. She presents and sustains the company's viewpoint during the organizational phase of the event. Her attendance at the meetings resulted in the decision to put the finish line in front of the company's new corporate headquarters.

TIME FRAME: Several months before the event.

ACTIVITY: Meetings are being held within the company to drum up volunteers, assign tasks, form relay teams, and set up such support activities as water stations.

TIME FRAME: About two weeks before the event.

ACTIVITY: The company (the client) likes the idea of sponsoring a disabled runner. Cyril Charles, a native of Trinidad and a blind marathon runner in training for the New York City Marathon, is contacted through the Achilles Track Club in New York. The club, which is dedicated to runners with disabilities of all kinds, sends press clips about their organization. This material becomes part of the press package developed for the client. Plans are made to bring Charles to the city a few days early to make him available to the media. A freelance consultant is assigned the task of generating favorable publicity.

TIME FRAME: Fourteen days before.

ACTIVITY: A brief public relations plan is written and an itinerary for Charles takes shape. The press release is drafted.

The press release is the most important public relations tool for any activity. It legitimizes your activity as a publicist or public relations professional and also names a contact. The release highlights facts about the event and creates interest in what is often a jaded audience.

The release must be approved by the client and anyone else involved with the event. This can take time. For the blind marathon runner, the release included the announcement of a public appearance (at the United Cerebral Palsy Association) as a way of giving the television crews something to photograph and of allowing Charles to share his experiences. Thus, the release had to be approved by the client and the United Cerebral Palsy Association.

Note that the United Cerebral Palsy Association is centrally located. Easy access is very important to the media because they have to cover lots of stories every day. That's why you see so many famous people interrupted by television cameras in airports.

TIME FRAME: Ten days before.

ACTIVITY: Approvals and distribution of press release.

TIME FRAME: Seven days before.

ACTIVITY: Approvals are slow in coming, so a courier company and taxicabs deliver the releases to the local television, print, and radio contact people. Telephone calls have already been made to learn the names and titles of the most important people in the target media. Moreover, calls made to one of the two major city newspapers indicated significant interest. In return for their enthusiasm, everyone agreed not to send the release to the rival newspaper until the first paper had published its interview with Charles.

TIME FRAME: Four days before.

ACTIVITY: Charles arrives in Rochester, checks into a hotel, and almost immediately is interviewed by Bill Flynn of WXXI—the public radio station. Half an hour later, he speaks to a group of people at the United Cerebral Palsy Association. No other media show up, in spite of some interest shown on the telephone by one television channel.

By now, telephone contact with the media has become a daily event, and another opportunity presents itself. Attempts to interest inner-city schools in having Charles talk to classes with disabled students have not been successful, but a teacher at a local private school (Harley) hears opportunity knocking, both for Charles and for her school. A plan is established to have 105 schoolchildren chase Charles around the soccer field once to make the equivalent of the marathon length, 26.2 miles. Constant contact with interested television assignment editors (for the week and the weekend) yields two channels, but photographers from both stations arrive late and the students have to be booted around the field one more time. The "walkers"—those who participated at their own pace with shoes untied—never really got into the event, but the overall television coverage is good. One of the students who chased Charles in that event accompanies him on his bicycle in the actual marathon.

One hour later, Charles is interviewed by a reporter for the evening paper (the *Times-Union*). Featured on the front page the following night, Charles is profiled for his courage and endurance. The cover photo came about by making a client executive available at a track that was convenient for the reporter and photographer. A call was made to assure access to the track, which is part of a local university.

Charles and the executive wear t-shirts that clearly identify the client, who was mentioned favorably in the coverage.

TIME FRAME: One day before.

ACTIVITY: The media opportunities have been harvested. Charles and the people who will accompany him practice together briefly. Charles is then driven to a nearby park to relax and enjoy himself. This is also a good time to consider, and plan to fix, all the things that could go wrong at the marathon.

TIME FRAME: The day of the event.

ACTIVITY: The final assignment is to photograph the event for local and trade publicity. By 8:30 A.M., the runners, led by three men in wheelchairs, have started. The photographer's car was towed while she worked. Friendly police and a cash card get the photographer in position by the six-mile mark. The day grows darker, it begins to rain, and a wonderful PR opportunity is threatened by nature. But Charles puts in a personal best of just over $3\frac{1}{2}$ hours.

TIME FRAME: Follow-up.

ACTIVITY: In addition to getting Charles back to the airport for home, getting the film processed, and writing a follow-up release to accompany selected photographs to the trade and local press, meetings were held with the client to discuss the results of the effort. A photo and caption was sent to the trade press and suitable newsletter photos and releases were mailed to the United Cerebral Palsy Association, the Harley School, and the Achilles Track Club. The client's company newsletter, which is mailed to customers, provides additional coverage.

2

Developing a Plan of Action

Experienced public relations practitioners make a distinction between those who shoot from the hip and those who take aim. The ones who shoot from the hip—those who operate without a plan of action—invariably spend much of their time reacting to situations as they arise. Somehow they never seem able to find the time to plan. Too many activities keep getting in the way.

These people may appear to be busy (in fact, they usually generate an enormous amount of work), but they are rarely as successful as those who take the time to focus, and that means formulating workable plans.

Planning is essential to the success of a public relations program. From part-time programs run by volunteers to corporate programs executed by huge staffs, the degree of success is directly related to how well that organization planned and coordinated its efforts.

When the Tobacco Institute announced the "Great American Welcome" a week before the American Cancer Society's 1988 "Great American Smokeout," they did so only after careful planning and research. The institute was armed with survey results that asserted smokers dine out more frequently than nonsmokers and order more wine and liquor, thus appealing directly to restaurateurs' pocketbooks. The group had two clear goals: to get businesses to display decals letting smokers know they are welcome, and to time its announcement to counteract the terrific amount of publicity generated by the Cancer Society's smokeout.

A written plan allows you to:

1. Set priorities.
2. Work toward realistic, well-defined goals.
3. Evaluate your work by a previously agreed-upon yardstick.
4. Justify the time you spend on projects. (It is also handy for those times when you have to explain why someone's pet project is not receiving your full attention.)

Looking at Your Organization: Research

Writing a public relations plan is impossible without first looking at your organization and its mission, establishing priorities, organizing activities, and anticipating results.

The first step in the planning process is to do basic research about your company or organization. Don't be intimidated by the word "research." Contrary to popular belief, research is not always expensive and time-consuming, and it's usually not something you'll have to hire a consultant to do. Informal research done by an in-house public relations person can be extremely revealing, and fairly easy to do. Research is also important in evaluating communications programs, and many of the techniques discussed here are used both before and after program implementation.

A survey conducted by Ketchum Public Relations shows how important research is in the field of public relations. Of 253 public relations professionals who responded to the survey, 32 percent agreed strongly and 44 percent agreed somewhat that research should be part of the planning, development, and evaluation of public relations. It's interesting to note that the research itself became part of Ketchum's public relations effort; the survey was released to the media and coverage included an editorial in *PR Week*.

Some of the best research is done when one or two people simply sit down and think about the organization. David Eisenstadt, president of a Toronto-based public relations firm, said in a recent article that "attitudes can often be determined simply by informed intuition."

The following section explains several research methods that are easy to execute and cost-effective.

Organizational Audits:
Internal and External

An organizational audit is an easy and informative re-search tool. To do an internal audit of the organization, that is, to measure how it sees itself, ask yourself the following questions:

- What are the company's/organization's strengths?
- What are its weaknesses?
- What exactly is affecting the company's bottom line, its success or failure?
- Why aren't earnings higher? How can they be improved?
- What is the quality of its products or services?
- Are employees effective at their jobs? Do they form a productive team?
- Is the organization a good corporate citizen? What does it do to enhance the community and environment?
- Is the company committed to quality? To fair prices?
- How is the organization different from what it was a year ago? Five years ago?
- Have people's attitudes toward it changed? How? Why?
- Where does the organization want to be in one year? In five years?
- In five years, what do you want people's attitudes toward the organization to be?

Once you've compiled your answers, ask several other people within the organization the same questions. Then coordinate their answers with yours.

To do an external audit, which researches how others (such as clients, customers, and neighbors) see the organization, ask a representative sampling the same questions.

Mail and Phone Analysis

A research method that measures external attitudes and can yield a great deal of information about your customers and clients, as well as the general business population, involves analyzing incoming mail and telephone calls. What kind of calls and letters does the organization get? Watch for letters and calls complaining about or praising the organization, especially in specifics. These reactions can help you determine how the general public perceives the organization.

Media Audits

To learn how the organization has been represented in the media, study past newspaper clippings. Look for trends in the coverage. Are there certain themes that run through the articles, regardless of who wrote them? Does a picture of the organization develop from how it has been portrayed in the media? Try to forget everything you know about the organization, and imagine how it would look to someone who knew it only from what had been presented in the news.

For a current look at media attitudes, clip all the articles about your organization, company, service industry, *and* its competitors that appear in local newspapers over a two-week period. During the same two-week period, take note of every television and radio news broadcast covering the same topics. (If the resources are available to you, assign staff members to monitor different stations.) This should give you a good look at how you, your service industry, and other organizations like yours are viewed (and portrayed) by the media.

It's possible that there won't be enough media coverage during the two-week period to be helpful. Or you might want to know how individual members of the media view the organization. Take the direct approach: Do a media audit, and simply call them up and ask. While you're at it, ask how they perceive your competitors. If you are diplomatic and convince members of the media that you are genuinely interested in their opinions, which indeed you should be, they may surprise you by their receptivity and candor.

Audience Identification: Who's Out There?

Set your research results aside for a moment and think about whom you want to influence through your public relations program. Is your target audience 12- to 24-

year-old white males? Middle-class married working mothers? Your overall audience may not be that simple to define and will probably be made up of several sub-groups.

Identifying those audiences is the key to the planning process. You can't develop an effectively targeted public relations program if you don't know whom to target. Identify your audience by making a list of every definable group that has any reason to be interested in or affected by your organization or company. Here, for example, are a few of the potential audiences for an up-and-coming art gallery located on the edge of an upper-class residential neighborhood:

- Local art patrons
- Area artists, including exhibitors in the gallery and artists who haven't shown their work at the gallery
- Artists from other disciplines, such as dance, theater, and music
- People who live in the neighborhood
- Other businesses in the neighborhood
- Other gallery owners/exhibitors
- Corporations and foundations that support the arts
- Newspaper, television, and radio art critics
- "Beat" reporters who cover your geographic area
- Students enrolled in the applied arts programs at local colleges

Some of the audiences will overlap, and others will

have only a tangential interest in your organization. In the above example, the gallery's neighbors have very different reasons for being interested in the gallery than do local art critics, but obtaining the goodwill of both groups is important.

Another method for identifying audiences is to analyze your organization's or company's mailing list. This is especially useful for nonprofit groups. Look at who is on the list, and why.

Mailing lists can add important demographic information to your research efforts. For example, if a large number of people on our art gallery's mailing list live in one suburban area, the gallery might choose to make a concentrated effort to get coverage in the weekly newspaper serving that area.

The Mission Statement

The information you've gathered is useless to you until you perform the next step in the planning process, which is to sift through the facts, perceptions, and attitudes you've amassed. Based on what you learn from this information, write a short statement that answers this question: What is the overall mission, or goal, of the organization/company?

The answer should be brief—just a few sentences—and written in clear and simple language. A mission statement for our art gallery might be: "To present fine art by outstanding area artists to the community at large, and to offer these works for sale at prices that are reasonable, yet high enough to help exhibitors support themselves through their artwork."

Notice that in this example the statement makes it clear that price is an issue, but not in terms of saving money for its customers. In this case, the gallery is presenting a mission statement that will enable it to justify high prices for contemporary art, because the gallery's stated mission includes helping artists earn a living without having to take second jobs to support their work.

The mission statement should include your organization's USP—its Unique Selling Point. This is the angle that makes your organization different, that makes it stand out from the crowd—the same angle that will make your public relations materials newsworthy.

Writing the Plan

A public relations plan can't be faked. You must know your organization or company, be able to evaluate problems, identify opportunities, and translate the information into a meaningful plan of action. We have included here, as a sidebar, the entire plan for the case history in Chapter 1. Writing a step-by-step plan of action is practically impossible if you have not first done some basic research.

There are as many formats for public relations plans as there are plans themselves. They all, however, share three sets of basic elements: situation and opportunity (goals) statements, strategies and tactics, and timeline and budget.

SAMPLE PLAN ●

PR Plan for RCI's Participation in the Rochester Marathon— October 2, 1988

OVERVIEW

This year, for the first time, RCI has chosen to participate in the Rochester Marathon. Effective public relations tactics will gain positive visibility for the company, in part because RCI has chosen to sponsor a blind marathon runner. The theme of "setting and achieving your own goals" is a good one both for Cyril Charles, the sponsored runner, and for RCI. Furthermore, many RCI employees will be participating in relays or encouraging runners along the route, providing a strong corporate presence.

OBJECTIVES

- To gain positive recognition for RCI and Cyril Charles in the local television, radio, and print media.

- To achieve RCI's visibility in the trade press.
- To publicize the marathon activities in the RCI customer newsletter.
- To create a bridge for possible publicity efforts in the New York City Marathon in early November.

TACTICS

1. Have Cyril Charles available for every media opportunity.
   Cyril in Rochester from September 29–October 2.
   Press release and fact sheet announcing RCI's participation.
   Media contact with electronic and print media.
   Possible outreach opportunity with disabled athletes and high school students.
2. Encourage press participation.
   Press bus to be discussed September 23 at committee meeting.
   Mobile phone dedicated to press use at registration table.
3. Capitalize on RCI sponsorship.
   Be sure all sponsored runners are clearly identified with RCI.
   New Rochester Telephone building to have a banner ("Marathon Service from RCI" or "RCI Goes the Distance").

TIMELINE

1. Press release and fact sheet for RCI approval: Thursday, September 22.

2. Release to Rochester media mailed September 23.

3. Banner on building September 29.

4. RCI shirts to runners October 2.

5. Caption and photography to trade press week of October 1.

6. Photos and short article in next issue of newsletter.

BUDGET

1. Estimated budget
   - Meetings with RCI—5 hours
   - Time in account handling, including transportation, training, and media contacts for Cyril Charles—20 hours
   - Writing press release, fact sheet, and photo caption—3 hours

TOTAL (account handling @ $30 per hour, writing @ $40 per hour): $870

Out-of-pocket expenses (long distance, fax, film): $30

Not included is the cost of photographic prints. Estimate at approximately $7.50 per print.

2. Banner 4 × 7 ft. $375–$400.

3. RCI runner's shirts: $116
   RCI visors: $222
4. Travel: $250
5. Hotel accommodations: $40 each night @ 3 =
$120
6. Meals (September 29–October 2): estimate $75
per day for two.
TOTAL: $2600

ITINERARY FOR CYRIL CHARLES

Arrives Thursday, September 29 9:57 A.M.
12:00 noon WXXI radio interview
1:30–2:30 P.M. talk to United Cerebral Palsy
3:00–4:00 P.M. interview with Mary Gay Johnson,
   Times-Union

Friday, September 30
12:00 noon meet companion for marathon
2:00–3:00 P.M. Harley School for one lap with 105
   students, Channels 10 and 13 record the event
4:00 P.M. meet RCI management

Saturday, October 1
Day-long trip to Letchworth Park

Sunday, October 2
8:00 A.M. Rochester Marathon
5:15 P.M. Rochester airport

ADDENDUM: Actual media response
- Cover story, *Times-Union*, Friday, September 30
- Multiple transmission of WXXI radio report
- Channel 10, 6:00 and 11:00 news, September 30
- Channel 13, 6:00 and 11:00 news, September 30
- Internal communications through RCI newsletter
- Mention in trade press

Situation and Opportunity Statements: Where You Are; Where You're Going

The situation statement briefly describes the situation you find yourself in, whether it be good or bad. The statement should contain no surprises. It succinctly states the key facts that are already known. It may also incorporate all or part of the mission statement you developed earlier, depending on the scope of the public relations program.

The opportunity, or program goals, statement responds to the situation. Ask yourself: What opportunity, or challenge, does this situation present? What can we do to take advantage of the situation? You may have to address several problems and from there several goals. In the case of our fictitious art gallery, one problem is a public perception that it is high priced and snobbish. The gallery might decide to address the problem through this goal: "To communicate the high value of the artwork exhibited."

Note that this goal acknowledges the gallery's high prices. *Public relations goals cannot change business realities.* Since prices can't be changed merely to make a public relations job easier, you must set a reasonable goal. In this case, the goal is to communicate why prices are high—because in return buyers get valuable artworks. The gallery could also choose a slightly different goal that stresses the investment value of contemporary art.

Some problems may not be directly related to your mission statement but arise during your research. For example, perhaps the gallery has a poor image in the neighborhood because of crowded, noisy opening-night receptions that disturb residents and take up their parking space.

Well-written public relations goals tackle problems and state them in a positive light—as opportunities. The problem of the opening-night reception can be put into positive terms quite simply: "To improve community relations."

Strategies: The Routes to Take

Never confuse strategies and goals. A goal, like the example above, is what you want to achieve in the long run, over a period of time. It is where you want to be at the end of the program.

A strategy is the specific route you take to get to that goal. A strategy to reach the goal of improving community relations might be: "To establish a working relationship with the neighborhood and create a means for ongoing communications and joint problem-solving."

Every goal should have at least one strategy, and media relations should have a separate strategy.

A media relations strategy might read:

> "To create ongoing relationships with art critics in the local media and receive coverage in all the major media."

Both examples of strategy statements incorporate a way to measure the success or failure of the strategy. In the first, the strategy states that the art gallery will "create a means for ongoing communications." In the second, the measurable aspect is expressed by the statement that the gallery intends to gain coverage in major media during the year.

Tactics: The Vehicles to Use

Tactics are the individual steps an organization or company takes to carry out its strategies and thus reach its goals. The tactics will serve as an outline of all public relations activities planned for the year.

For example, when Ketchum Public Relations wrote its plan for the survey of public relations professionals mentioned earlier in this chapter, one of the tactics listed was probably "release survey results to the media." Taking a step back for a moment, the strategy statement that this tactic follows might have been "to strengthen Ketchum's image as an important source of in-depth information on the field of public relations." Other tactics could include sending out press releases that position employees as experts in certain areas, such as financial public relations, for media interviews.

Each tactic should include a timeline and estimated budget. Although you may not be able to adhere strictly to the timeline or budget because of unforeseen circumstances (a sudden rise in the cost of paper, for example, can significantly affect the cost of producing a newsletter), they will help you stay on track during the year.

Tactics should be concrete, measurable, and achievable. Let's go back to the art gallery. We already have the basis of a full public relations plan: mission statement, goals, and strategies. Now for some tactics:

- Join the neighborhood association, attend meetings, and become active on at least one committee.
- Hold two receptions for neighbors only, where they can meet artists and tour the gallery.
- Announce opening-night receptions in the neighborhood association newsletter, listing times and dates so neighbors can be prepared for the extra traffic in the area.

• Make arrangements for alternative parking nearby and post clear, easily readable directions to the lot.

As this list shows, each strategy may have several tactics. Once good relations with the community have been established and the neighborhood has become an ally, the gallery may want to include an article in its newsletter about its successful community relations effort and suggest such an article to the local media or to a magazine that covers art institutions.

Timeline and Budget: Keeping on Track

The timeline and budget are critical elements of your communications plan. Both show your intentions in carrying out the program: when you will execute tactics and how much you expect to spend on each one.

The smartest way to write a timeline is to begin at the end—the date of the event or when the tactic will be completed—and work backwards from there. Be sure to give yourself plenty of time for each step. It's better to have too much time than too little.

To make the budget as accurate as possible, we suggest getting actual cost estimates from the suppliers you will be using.

When you have completed the timeline, keep it handy and refer to it often. Use it as a reminder of what you need to be doing to keep the program on schedule.

CASE HISTORY ●

Introducing "Choc-Eez" to the World

It's Monday morning, and the president of your company has called you into his office to tell you that a new product, chocolate toothpaste, is going to be introduced to the public next month. The people in marketing have decided to call the toothpaste "Choc-Eez." Your job is to create a public relations program to help introduce the product.

Let's assume the marketing staff has already done the research, so you know the target audience, its tastes, attitudes, and demographics, as well as the advantage of your product. All you have to do is write the plan.

Here's a sample plan. It's not as detailed as an actual plan would be. Note that the situation and opportunity statements are used to summarize the data already known, point out why the information is important, and in general set the scene for the rest of the program.

SITUATION: A new chemical process invented in our company's research lab enabled us to add real chocolate to toothpaste without promoting tooth decay. No other toothpaste company has been able to do this, although we believe one or two may be close to a breakthrough.

This product fills a clearly identified need for parents trying to encourage young children to brush their teeth. The addition of mint and other flavors has not satisfied children's taste buds; nearly all children up to age ten hate to brush their teeth and consider it a chore and a form of punishment.

Adolescents and adults, particularly single women 20 to 40 years old, also responded favorably to the toothpaste. A major product benefit, in their minds, is that it is low in calories and does not promote either weight gain or acne. Some, however, were skeptical and did not believe these benefits were possible.

OPPORTUNITY: To broaden our product line to include a new, unique health-care product that was created using the advanced research capabilities of our company.

STRATEGIES: To introduce "Choc-Eez" to a broad cross section of the general population, including parents of young children, children, teens, and unmarried professional women.

To communicate the dental-care benefits and unique characteristics of "Choc-Eez" to both the public and dental-care professionals.

To gain widespread attention from national, regional, local, and consumer-oriented media.

To gain extensive coverage in the dental trade press.

TACTICS: Develop a media list and create a press kit geared to general-interest media.

Develop a dental trade press media list and create a press kit geared specifically to their needs.

Produce product photography for use in press kits and in individual articles.

Execute a media tour to trade press editors. (This involves hitting the road with an expert or two from your company and setting up meetings to discuss the product face to face, usually at the editors' offices.)

Place bylined articles in trade publications, highlighting in-depth research, testing of the new product and outstanding product benefits. Also, place an article discussing how dentists can enhance their practice by using and promoting the use of "Choc-Eez."

Identify and attend appropriate dental and candy industry trade shows. Make contacts with trade editors and other media covering the show.

These are just a few ideas; there are many, many, more. The public relations person assigned to "Choc-Eez" might try to get a celebrity spokesperson (a child, naturally) on the early-morning talk shows, to produce a newsletter to dentists aimed at increasing awareness of the product, or to develop a video news release about kids and teeth. The list can only be limited by time, energy, and budget resources.

You would end the plan with a timeline and a budget.

3

Evaluating Your PR Program

Establishing Accountability

Public relations can do many things to improve communication in every part of business and social life, but the one thing it does with difficulty is to give a measurable account of its own success. Because employers and clients like to see results for the work they are funding, however, it is essential to find a way to show proven, measurable results.

"Management by objectives" has made accountability the basis of every modern business transaction and communications program, including public relations. The foremost question in management's mind is, "What am I getting for my money?" This is why evaluation must be built into every public relations program you undertake, using both qualitative (what?) and quantitative (how much?) methods. It won't be sufficient just to say that people feel better because of the brochure they received. And even if you are part of a completely volunteer public relations committee, your plans will require some budget allowance, if only for printing and postage. When money is allocated, the funding source expects that it will be spent wisely and effectively.

Evaluating the effectiveness of your communications program is an essential part of your job as a public relations professional. You need to know, for example, what kind of results you are achieving, if management is aware and appreciative of your effort, how your function is understood by others in your company or organization, and if you're getting the budget you need to carry out your program.

Though answering these questions is vital to the success of your program, it is not an easy assignment. Consider the difficulty in determining attitudes, especially on sensitive topics. It has been widely reported, for example, that when surveyed about their sexual habits most Americans do not tell the truth. Furthermore, it is also hard to determine if a reporter covered a topic because you sent a press release about it six months before the story appeared. Or that $10,000 videotape—did it help employees understand why the company they were working for had just been acquired by another company, one they never heard of? And that in a mass mailing, which may go to every major metropolitan newspaper and television station in the country, it is impossible, even with an excellent clipping service, to receive credit for each and every placement gained.

A public relations program is easier to evaluate if you plan to evaluate it from the beginning. Then you can incorporate and use elements of the program as built-in evaluation tools. A direct-mail piece with a reply card, for example, already contains a measurement device for program evaluation.

A few public relations firms think they have found a computer solution to accountability. Some public relations practitioners have designed complicated computer tracking systems to help evaluate the effectiveness of their media placements. They award a certain amount of points for the number of inches of print their client gets, the headline size, the general tone of the article, and its physical placement in the newspaper, on television, or on radio. A positive cover or lead story gets the highest number of points.

This approach, however, can be only as good as the information sustaining it. Paper sophistication alone can't substitute for the nuts and bolts of public relations work—writing, interviewing, researching, rewriting, calling editors, working with other professionals, arranging special events, following up.

Quantitative Measurement: Proving It's Working

Until the early 1980s, the established way to prove the effectiveness of a public relations program was with a "clip book"—a collection of your newspaper and magazine clippings, radio mentions, and a reel of your television placements.

With print clips, the statistics that count are the number of placements, circulation (including the number of people reached by the placement), demographics, geographic distribution, and the equivalent value in advertising cost. No matter how sophisticated public relations becomes as a profession, this kind of qualitative measurement will still be the basis of measuring results. But it is a little behind the times to use it as the only method.

Qualitative Measurement: Beyond the Numbers

A public relations professional once described a public relations program that, on paper, seemed to promise excellent results. The goal of the program was to increase public awareness of the need for street lighting, and the public relations staff was thrilled to count the number of inches they received in the press. The papers that covered the issue, however, were located in small rural communities where street lighting was highly unlikely to be found, so in reality the public relations efforts accounted for little in effective results.

The moral of this story: Don't count your inches until you can also determine that you have reached the target market and that the market will respond. Probably the most intelligent measure for accountability is the "call to action"—some device that *asks* the target audience to respond. For example, if you are promoting the new Go to Fitness health club with a direct-mail campaign, you can tabulate the response cards and count the number of people who said yes to the offer.

Maybe you represent an organization that is launching an annual fund drive, or a group looking for new members, or an environmental group that needs increased publicity to gain political support. The effectiveness of the public relations effort quickly becomes obvious if more money was raised, new people joined, or if politicians began to ask for the group's opinions.

Proven Evaluation Tools

Here are some traditional public relations tools to help you evaluate your communications program.

Pre-/Post-Testing

Pre-testing is necessary to determine if the proposed project will reach and influence its intended audience. Because pre-testing is done before a project is committed to or produced, it is usually inexpensive to perform. It can also save time and money.

For example, to pre-test an upcoming brochure for hearing-impaired alcoholics, the public relations person asked a control group of deaf drinkers to read the copy before proceeding with the production and distribution of the brochure.

Post-testing is conducted afterwards, and although it will not save an already completed project, it will help you avoid repeating mistakes if your communications were off-target. Even pre-tested projects should be post-tested to refine materials further. The responses of an entire group of hearing-impaired alcoholics to the initial brochure were used to create more and better communications tools.

The tools of pre- and post-testing are well recognized among advertising professionals. What petrochemical company wants to spend a million dollars on a television ad for a new pesticide aimed at farmers only to find out that farmers listen to the early-morning stock report on the radio instead?

Testing is just as important during or after a public relations event. A telecommunications long-distance carrier recently spent $900 sending cheesecakes to each regional office to celebrate the tenth anniversary of its hardware business. A photo of top management cutting cheesecake was published in the trade press, which was great, but did the employees feel honored? No one knows. If it had done some testing, using a random telephone survey or by making quick-reply cards available at the cake cuttings, the company could have surveyed employee attitudes before and after the event. Depending on those results, it would be easier to justify a similar program the following year, or to recommend to management that it save $900 since attitudes did not seem to improve significantly.

Controlled Market Comparison

Large organizations with big communications budgets like to compare one public relations format to another. This might mean comparing a communications program with public relations support to a program without support as part of a controlled market comparison.

Let's go back to the "Choc-Eez" introduction, the new chocolate-flavored toothpaste aimed at children. Market test sites are established on the East Coast and in southern Florida. In one market, public relations will be used, along with advertising and sales promotion, to launch the product. In the other market, public relations is not part of the launch plan. What you would determine is whether using public relations justifies its cost.

If you are with a nonprofit organization, you can modify this idea to test your effectiveness. Let's say, for example, that you are part of a recruitment program for area youth groups. Try a concentrated public relations effort in one neighborhood and do no public relations in a similar neighborhood. Once the results are in, in terms of market penetration, you can compare them to the cost of producing the public relations.

Direct Response

When book buyers mention that they heard about a book on the "Today" show, they are making a direct-response statement. Other direct-response vehicles are reply cards and warranty cards that the customer mails back to the manufacturer.

Publicity on the "Today" show is an extremely cost-effective way to build book sales. The "Today" show, in fact, has been cited as the premier place to publicize a book. Why is it better than "Good Morning America"? Who knows? It could have something to do with the demographics of those who watch the programs.

A successful direct-response program led to the recent demise of Batman's sidekick, Robin. DC comics listed a telephone number for a two-day telephone poll in an issue of the popular comic book, asking readers to vote on whether Robin should live or die after being injured in an explosion. Reader response was excellent—10,614 people called—and more publicity was gained through coverage of the results. Robin was bumped off by a margin of 72 votes.

The Communications Audit: Taking a Picture of the "Bigger Picture"

The purpose of a communications audit is to learn more about how organizations and businesses communicate and to plan for improved productivity. The benefits are twofold: (1) being able to identify strengths and weaknesses to help determine which areas of a communications program need work, and (2) establishing a base against which to measure future results. One public relations consultant recommends a communications audit every two to five years, or when significant external or internal events occur, including mergers, acquisitions, changes in management, corporate reorganization, union negotiations, or economic changes.

Although a communications audit, professionally done, can typically cost $10,000 to $13,000 in fees and $2,000 to $3,000 in out-of-pocket expenses, it can pay for itself if it shows how to eliminate unnecessary or ineffective communications efforts, and if it strengthens existing efforts and saves time and effort. The biggest liability of a public relations program is to make an assumption, without testing, about what the target audience thinks.

A small business or organization can conduct its own audit, but we recommend that any questionnaire used be developed with professional help to avoid asking questions that "lead" the person being interviewed and cause the results to be skewed. A low-cost alternative to hiring experts is to ask an instructor in public relations or marketing at a local college to produce the audit for you, either as a freelance project or an assignment for a marketing class.

Steps in Making the Audit

1. What do you hope to accomplish? Will the survey be internal (within the company or organization), or will it be limited to or include external publics as well (for example, sponsors, media representatives, neighbors, competitive organizations, people who chose not to join your group)?

2. What are your objectives? What do you hope to gain from the audit? Include the overall objectives as well as the objectives for specific elements of the public relations program. For example, specific objectives would be to save money, to gain awareness, and to increase membership.

3. What ways can you develop to measure such factors as resources, target groups, and financial activities?

4. How will you conduct the audit and collect the data? Observation, questionnaire, interview, interception, mail, and telephone are all traditional methods used in an audit, often in combination, depending on the group you hope to reach.

5. How will you analyze and interpret the data obtained?

6. What form will your recommendation take, and how will you share it with others? Often a communications audit is presented to management as a series of reports. In this way, the information is easy to comprehend and goals can be changed if necessary.

7. Most important, will the results bring about change? Results will be more effective in bringing about change if management is invested in the communications audit from the very beginning. Recommendations must be expressed in "action items" or ways that strongly suggest follow-through. A series of follow-up reports, made regularly, is one way to achieve positive, constructive change from what you've learned.

Who Will Be Surveyed?

The various publics routinely surveyed in a communications audit are:

- Internal staff, from CEO to maintenance, representing all departments.
- A random sampling of members, clients, or customers.
- A random list of prospects or a target audience for future business transactions.
- Rejectors—people whom you approached with your product or service but who chose not to participate.
- Appropriate specifiers of your service, meaning people in a position to recommend your service to others.
- Local, regional, and national media appropriate to the way you do business.

Internal Audits

The internal audit is done first in order to establish the issues. Begin by developing an audit plan with time-lines. Then conduct interviews with top management of your company or organization to survey attitudes and to identify problems.

Next, collect, inventory, and analyze communications materials, such as brochures, newsletters, press releases, and a calendar of events.

Now come the internal audiences—employees and staff members. Establish focus groups and conduct individual interviews with randomly selected representatives of these audiences. This will help you identify attitudes and concerns and to develop a questionnaire that will give you the data you need.

Prepare the questionnaire for internal audiences and share it with management before you use it. It is imperative to the success of the program that management feels involved every step of the way. Now, test the questionnaire on control groups to detect possible flaws, such as with language; perhaps the questions are not appropriate to the audience.

When you are satisfied that the questionnaire will be effective, administer it to internal audiences in person in focus groups, by telephone, or through the mail.

Tabulate and summarize responses. Then report the results quickly and candidly to management and the internal audiences as well, both verbally and with a written follow-up.

External Audits

Auditing external audiences—those outside the company or organization, such as the media, competing groups, the general public, and community leaders—is a similar procedure. The big difference between internal and external audits is the type of questions asked. First, do some research to help prepare the questionnaire. Look at news clips, literature, and information about competing or similar organizations.

Next, identify your external audiences. This could include community leaders, former members of your company or organization, people who learned about your group but decided not to join (the "rejectors"), sponsors, and local news media.

Now conduct focus groups and interviews with external audiences, chosen at random, to help in the preparation of the questionnaire. Remember, you are looking for opinions and attitudes; let these people be your guide. After preparing and testing the questionnaire, distribute it in person, by telephone, through questioners at malls ("mall intercepts"), or by mail.

Finally, tabulate and summarize your results by analyzing and interpreting your data. Use this information to prepare and present a cumulative series of interim reports to management and to your internal audiences. The result should be recommendations for action items and follow-through.

A two- to four-year communications plan could result from a communications audit. It would include:

- A statement of goals and objectives
- Identification of key audiences
- An analysis of key audiences' attitudes and opinions
- Appropriate channels for reaching those publics
- Messages and themes to stress one- and three-year budgets
- Action steps
- A method of evaluating results

Avoiding Audit Pitfalls

You can improve your chances for success—that is, gaining meaningful information about your organization or company that will enhance your communications—with these suggestions:

1. Sell management on the idea with a crisp presentation that emphasizes the benefits of doing an audit: improving communications with key publics, ensuring the efficiency of future communications budgets, and creating an information base for long-range communications planning.

2. Gain management approval for all questionnaires and the interview slate.

3. Sell your public relations staff on the value of an audit before you begin. You need their help and support. Keep them informed and consult with them at every step.

4. Choose the right time—never during or after labor-management confrontations, for instance, and at least six months after you've been on the job.

5. Conduct an audit when other large projects are not crowding the schedule. Remember, senior management must be invested in the process in order for the results to effect change.

6. Conduct internal interviews first, because the information you receive will help you determine who your external audiences are and what questions to ask them.

7. Keep information and opinions you receive private and confidential.

8. Keep the questions open-ended and nonthreatening. Every group has sensitivities, so be careful in your approach. Don't ask, for example, "How is morale in your department?" Try, instead, "What do you do to maintain a positive and productive attitude?"

9. Don't rush. Give the interviewees as much time as they need to answer your questions. Some people take longer than others to get their ideas flowing.

10. Keep your opinions to yourself.

11. Don't let an audit drag on and on. Timeliness is vital so that the project is viewed as important to the overall group.

12. Be sure to act in some way upon the report findings. Otherwise a communications audit winds up as an empty exercise.

4

Tools of the Trade: Press Releases, Newsletters, Brochures, and More

What is Public Relations Writing?

Public relations writing follows established journalistic standards and style. The reason is simple: The less an editor has to do to your release to make it conform to the paper's style, the more likely he or she is to use your materials. This is especially true of smaller, weekly newspapers and the business section of daily papers.

Even if you don't want the editor to run your story "as is," you still have a responsibility to prepare information in a style and format that is standard in the profession and therefore easy for the editor to handle. Each week, an editor or reporter at a medium-sized daily newspaper sees hundreds of press releases. So do counterparts at the local television and radio stations. It's your job to make it as easy as possible for them to evaluate your release. If you don't, you're likely to be disregarded when the time comes to assign the day's stories.

Press Releases: What They Can Do

A press, or news, release is the basic format for getting a message to your intended audience. It is a relatively short announcement of new products, policies, pricing changes, events, personnel moves, and other timely information of interest to your audience(s) and/or the general public. A press release opens the door for the actual media contact.

The press release's purpose is to inform and interest the reader on topics that range from congressional legislation updates, mall openings, medical and scientific discoveries, the announcement of new products to the trade (just think of the flood of releases that announced the cola wars!), to such details as what people wore to a cocktail party and what they ate. In a recent flap, for example, over whether or not a certain gossip columnist attended a certain cocktail party, the warring faction (another gossip columnist who insists he *did* attend the party) charged that the first columnist got her information from a press release.

Press releases are versatile, serving many different purposes. For example, a background release can tell people about your product or service in depth and in relation to the industry as a whole, while a personnel release announces your new hire, listing his or her qualifications and credentials. (When accompanied by a photograph, the personnel release is probably the second most likely release to find placement on the business pages of the local and trade press. The first most likely format is a well-conceived letter to the editor.)

Press releases are written in standard "newspaper style"—including who, what, where, when, how, and what's happening—so that they can be published with a minimum of editing and fit easily into a limited space. The writing should be as clear, accurate, and concise as you can make it.

Usually press releases are sent simultaneously to all appropriate magazines, newspapers, and television and radio stations. The release may be used by print, radio, and television media in several ways: as submitted; as a calendar listing; or as the basis for a short article, feature, or detailed coverage by a reporter. To create interest, write about user-related benefits and offer solutions to problems rather than simply listing product features. And it's fine to supply appropriate quotes for people—they add reader interest. (Note, however, that quotes are most effective in the second or third paragraph of a press release.)

When writing the release, avoid the first person and do not editorialize. An opinion is appropriate only for a person who represents your organization or one who is an authority in the field and should be a direct quotation.

After we formed the idea for this book, we wrote a press release announcing its availability, including an outline and sample chapter. The release explained what we hoped to accomplish by writing the book and included our credentials. We also made sure to mention that *Books in Print* did not list another book like the one we proposed. We sent the release to ninety publishers and got a positive response from nearly one-third—demonstrating that the release was an effective response getter.

Parts of a Press Release

LETTERHEAD. News release or company letterhead. Type "News Release" if you are using company letterhead

RELEASE DATE. For Immediate Release (typed at the top of the page)

CONTACT(S). Name, title, telephone number(s)

Type the release date and contacts in the upper-right corner. Indicate one or two persons an editor can contact for further information or clarification. Include full names (titles when appropriate), telephone numbers, and best times of day the persons can be reached. (If the editor works at night, for example, a contact for evening hours is important.)

Be sure that the person (you or someone else) listed as the contact knows about the release, has agreed to be a contact, and supports all communications objectives.

DATELINE. Appears at the beginning of the first paragraph of the release and gives the place where the release originates and the date. Its use is optional.

BODY. The release is double spaced, with indented paragraphs (no extra space between paragraphs). Allow wide, wide margins on both sides. Editors need room to make notes. If you use a word processor or computer, choose a type style that is easy to read.

Keep paragraphs short, no more than two or three sentences each. Follow standard journalistic practice for capitalization, punctuation, and general style.

Title each page after the first page. You can do this by shortening the headline to form an identifier and then adding the page number. At the end of the release, type #, ###, or "end." If the release continues for more than one page, write "–more–" at the bottom of the first and all continuing pages.

The final item on a press release is the editor's note. Use it sparingly—when you want to direct information that would be of interest only to the editor, such as the time and location of a press conference. Or, use it when you have a specific message for the editor that should not be part of the release.

HEADLINES. Get the meat of the message in the head. For example, "Lodestar Corporation Announces New Product" is not as good as "Copy Ready in Two Minutes with Lodestar's New Copier." The length of the headline is important, too—eight to fifteen words is recommended. Headlines can be typed flush left or centered.

The following suggestions will help you produce a crisp, clearly written press release. Press releases that are well written and attractively presented are more likely to be used, regardless of the subject.

1. Keep the release concise. Type or word-process it double spaced on $8\frac{1}{2}$ × 11-inch good-quality white paper. No onionskin; it's hard to read. No colored paper or ink, either. Leave generous margins on all sides. Use only one side of the paper.

2. Include the most important information—who, what, when, where, why and how—in the first two paragraphs.

3. Provide complete and accurate information about everything you mention—the address (include the ZIP code), dates, exact times, titles, and sources of all quotations.

4. When writing about an event, be sure to give the date, time, place, and admission charge, if any. (If there is no charge, state that as well.) It's also important to mention if the event is accessible to the handicapped or if it will be interpreted in sign language for the hearing impaired.

5. Be sure you have all approvals that are necessary to send the press release out into the world: anyone mentioned in the release, company or organization officials, legal advisers, and all others likely to have an

interest. Keep all approvals on file in case somebody has a change of heart after the release is sent. (You'd be surprised how often this happens.)

6. Before sending the release, ask yourself: Does the press release clearly describe the event, activity, announcement, or accomplishment? Does it sound as if it could be of interest to someone not familiar with what's happening? Does the release answer any question the reader is likely to ask? If you answer no to any of these questions, revise the release until all the answers are yes.

7. Keep a copy of the release handy in case the editor or media calls to express an interest in your story. Be sure all contacts who might be called by the media have a copy as well. If the event is a press conference, have enough copies of the release to distribute to the press just prior to the conference.

Newsletters: Cost-Effective and Efficient

After the press release, newsletters are probably the most common form of communications vehicle used by the public relations professional. They offer an efficient and inexpensive way to inform and interest a select audience.

Many public relations practitioners believe that newsletter writing is an art form, best left to the specialists. We beg to differ. Most entry-level public relations positions, especially those in nonprofit organizations, involve newsletter writing. Newsletters are no more mysterious than press releases. In fact, the same basic rules apply: include all the pertinent information, organize articles well, write clearly, and target the information to the intended audience.

Newsletters are used by groups and organizations as a cost-effective, efficient way to reach an intended audience—employees, members, alumni, dealers, consumers, employees—any group, in fact, that would respond to and be motivated by information that is useful to them. Though they haven't the glamour and prestige of a glossy company magazine or corporate annual report, newsletters are an indispensable tool for informing and influencing many different kinds of readerships on many levels. Nonprofit groups find them to be indispensable as a way of communicating with volunteers and contributors.

You, as the public relations person, are usually responsible for the entire operation, including deciding the size and format, gathering the material, doing the interviews, writing the stories, supervising the production, and making sure the newsletters get mailed on time to the chosen or established readership. Have an art director or graphic designer format the information to make it more professional and interesting.

The newsletter layout and schedule is often demanding. If the schedule is for a monthly or even a quarterly publication, you always have a newsletter in the production cycle. The usual lead time for a newsletter is four to six weeks (from ideas through distribution), depending on the method of mechanical reproduction. If you need to conduct interviews first, the copy gathering alone could take two to three weeks.

The rule in writing newsletters is to focus continually on the reader. For example, a dealer sales letter will sound different than a fund-raising report. And you will probably find yourself writing for at least two—or more—categories of readership. The writing style usually follows standard journalistic practice, but you can fine-tune it to fit the audience.

The typical newsletter is $8\frac{1}{2}$ inches wide by 11 inches deep; four pages is a common length. Many organizations leave the outside bottom third blank for mailing address and postage: that's called a self-mailer.

Depending on the format—layout, type size, and style—a four-page newsletter requires about 3,000 words of copy. A variety of topics and article lengths will help add interest. Topics typically covered in a newsletter include: company sales and bottom line; updates on company personnel; new products and the intended market; application stories about users having good results with your product; user tips; holiday-oriented articles; and, if you are academic or nonprofit, fund-raising articles and features on alumni or services.

If the newsletter is for employees, consider including stories about the company itself. Employees want to know how their company is doing, and they want to know about other departments and divisions within the company. Make sure the newsletter is balanced, not leaning too heavily toward either business or people stories.

The most well-read articles in a newsletter are about people. Newsletters are one area where employees' outside interests might provide relevant copy. Gathering the information also gives you, the public relations professional, insight into the company or organization, as well as an opportunity to talk to everyone on staff. Newsletters also have specific columns that appear in each issue ("From the President's Desk," promotions, good housekeeping, safety, etc.).

The most important factor in producing a newsletter, however, and the one determining whether the newsletter is read, is timeliness. If you have to choose between useful news and perfection, always choose being useful and relevant to your readership. For news that breaks just at deadline, include the news as a bulletin-board display, then elaborate on it in a subsequent issue.

Credibility and readability are also important. Articles with the most credibility are factual and thoroughly and accurately researched. You will come to identify people in your company or organization who prove to be knowledgeable and reliable. These are your best contacts for news.

If you are lucky, you will have an art director, graphic designer, or desktop publisher who will help you to design a format and lay out (arrange) the pages. Whoever you are working with, keep the design clean and uncluttered. Don't mix many different type styles. Be direct in your format as well as in your text.

The most readable newsletters have two columns of copy on the page. A distinctive design, or logo, for the masthead and a catchy name help give the newsletter a distinct personality. Companies often hold contests to name newsletters, which is how Carborundum Abrasives employees decided to call their newsletter "The Sand Paper."

Photography is the preferred visual medium in a newsletter, but you need good, clear photographs and production by a professional printshop to get an acceptable image. Now entering the market, however, are copier products and desktop publishing systems using scanning devices that will help provide low-cost, quality reproduction of illustrations and photographs.

If you do not want to use photographs, or you want to supplement them, art supply houses have what is called "clip art"—illustrations depicting certain general themes that you can clip and use in the newsletter to add interest.

Photos and Captions

Photo captions are important because they enhance and highlight a communications piece. In fact, they're often what the reader will look at first. The captions should be brief, clearly identify every person pictured (moving from right to left or from left to right), and describe what is going on in the picture. They highlight the article without repeating the information in the text.

For style, take a look at *National Geographic*, where the captions come close to poetry. By reading only the captions, the reader usually can get a good idea of the entire story before reading the text.

Type the photo captions halfway down the page, one caption to a page. Tape the caption to the back of the photo about halfway down so that it appears just below the photograph. Fold the caption sheet to cover and protect the photograph in transit.

Never fold or bend a photograph. Add a stiffener, such as a piece of thin cardboard, to the envelope. Clearly label the outside of the envelope to indicate that it contains a photograph.

Brochures: Information and Persuasion

A brochure describes a product or service and what that product or service can do for the reader. Nonprofit organizations, for example, use brochures to educate consumers, describe services in a health maintenance organization, list tourist attractions in a particular area, explain organizational goals and achievements, or present volunteer opportunities in a community.

As a category of sales literature, brochures are used by companies to confirm customer expectations that they are in business, provide information the consumer can take home, and give the sales force a reinforcing selling tool. Employers use them to explain personnel policies and train their employees. When brochure copy is written by advertising rather than public relations staff, it is generally referred to as "collateral."

The Image Piece: Brochures for the Long Term

The capabilities brochure, company magazine, and annual report are examples of the image piece—one designed to establish a corporate or organizational position over a period of time. The capabilities brochure provides an overview of the product or service being offered. It describes the company or organization in terms of its history, its philosophy and goals, and its people, using its services, accomplishments, corporate structure, research and development, and major markets. What sets the annual report apart is that it represents the bottom line, with specific figures and statistics.

Depending upon the intended use, capabilities brochures might be included in press kits, mailed to employees, given to new employees, sent to stockholders, or used on sales calls to help set the stage in a prospect's mind.

Some companies have introduced company magazines that are similar to the capabilities brochure but augmented with stories about product applications and eye-catching covers. *Philip Morris* magazine has one of the largest circulations of any magazine in the United States. Corporations such as Kodak and Du Pont also have magazines, as do several computer and automobile companies. Crisco shortening even has a single-sponsor magazine, distributed in beauty salons in the South, that is designed to sell lard to home-makers.

Annual Reports

The annual report is the showpiece—usually the most expensive image piece a company or organization will publish in a year. For a large corporation, such as General Motors, the annual report could run forty pages or more. Although one study indicated that most investors spend only six minutes reading the annual report, those may be the most important six minutes in the relationship between investor and invested.

The annual report may be the most sensitive corporate or organizational document you ever help produce, as it includes summary, earnings disclosures, and reports required by the federal government. Because premature disclosure of information it contains could affect earnings and contributions, it is usually done in house by company employees. It is becoming increasingly commonplace to be candid about poor earnings or otherwise problem years.

Annual reports tend to be slick, full-color productions, with outstanding photography and computer-generated graphics. On the average, companies spend about $3 for each report. The 11,000 publicly held companies in the United States spent $5.1 billion in 1987 on annual reports, or an average of $463,000 each. Annual reports for nonprofit organizations are often more modest.

Tips on Producing a Brochure

Here are some guidelines for producing a brochure:

Understand how the brochure will be used. Will it be included in a direct-mail campaign, left after a sales call, handed out at a trade show, distributed to an interested audience, used as point-of-sale literature, or mailed to prospects who make inquiries? It should not duplicate, without improving, existing material.

The intended use of the brochure is the most important factor in determining how to present the information in terms of how much the reader needs to know (or already knows) about your product. Brochures that are intended to be image-building rather than instructional have a lot of text, while others use many photographs and drawings, a lot of white space (margins), and a minimum number of words.

Determine the size and format of the brochure by its intended use or readership. If your product or service is for a heavy industrial user, a pocket-size brochure with specifications might be ideal. Purchasing agents, for example, tend to use three-ring binders, so your layout should allow space for the holes. For a consumer product, an oversize, glossy, four-color treatment may help your product stand out from the crowd. A nonprofit organization, however, should be cautious about producing a brochure that looks expensive—unless, of course, a sponsor underwrote the project. In that case, be sure to give the sponsor a prominently placed credit line to acknowledge the contribution.

Adding a pocket to the brochure where more information sheets can be added is helpful. Being different can be attention getting, but it may also get your brochure thrown away. People like to file information in a standard-size ($8\frac{1}{2} \times 11$ inch) folder and may find a different size or shape cumbersome.

Your writing style as well will be determined by your audience. Some brochures are written in an informal style, presenting testimonies, case histories, and other examples focusing on people. Others stress factual material, using statistics, charts, and graphs. Study the competitive literature used in the market or service you are targeting.

Organize your material in a logical presentation that is easy to follow. Each page should be convincing and attractive by itself. Check your content for clear instructions to the reader on how to respond if interested—called, in marketing terms, "closing the sale." At some point, usually in the last few pages, you will want to lead the reader to take some kind of action. Make that move as easy as you can by prominently positioning the specific information, such as prices and terms, a distributor list, an 800 or other telephone number, a reply card, or some other response vehicle. Highlight guarantees and any other pertinent information.

The visual content can be photographs or illustrations, or both. A surprising number of well-written brochures are marred by poorly conceived and executed visuals. Use professional talent for illustration whenever your budget allows, and limit illustration to those images that support the text. All visuals should have explanatory captions.

Graphs, charts, diagrams, and maps can be used to condense information in a limited space. To make these data even more interesting visually, use computer graphics. By using a computer to enhance images, your brochure will appear modern and up to date; even a pie chart can become exciting. Computer graphics firms are listed in the Yellow Pages.

Sidebars, material highlighting points made in the text and featuring short lists of major benefits or features, draw reader attention to key selling points.

Design the cover to provide excitement and to present your strongest selling point—usually the promise of a benefit or solution to readers so that they will be motivated to read the brochure to the last page.

Other Public Relations Formats

Catalogues

Catalogues are similar to brochures but are more specific and focused. They present short, pithy descriptions of a product and are written in a crisp, condensed style to give as much information in as few words as possible.

You need to include all the information about the product, as well as help the reader make a decision in favor of buying the product described. The ordering information must be clear, consistent, and complete. In the product descriptions, use attention-getting words, emphasize the benefits, and don't hesitate to liven up the copy by using descriptive adjectives. Looking at mail-order catalogues is a good place to begin. These often have at the beginning of the piece a letter from the owner talking about the quality of the products, the reputation for service, and the employees. This letter helps personalize what is basically a sales tool with an order form attached.

Fact Sheets

Fact sheets are brief nuggets of important technical background information. The style and tone of the writing serves as an additional motivation to sales. Fact sheets can be included in the packaging with the product or service, in the press kit, or at the point of sale.

Fact sheets are usually one page, 8½ by 11 inches. They should be limited to one product per sheet. To organize your technical information, use bullets (•) or asterisks (*) to list the details that support the benefit or feature you are writing about.

Fact sheets are heavily used by nonprofit organizations because they are excellent for summarizing all programs or services. They often accompany press releases in place of background pieces or full press kits.

Flyers

Flyers, also called broadsides, are 8½ by 11-inch single-sheet handouts. They announce sales, new products, events, services, or new locations and often contain coupons. They are an inexpensive, effective way to reach new prospects. You see flyers nailed to telephone poles, taped on walls, or stuffed under the windshield wiper of your car. They are also used as handouts at trade shows, supermarkets, and shopping malls.

Invoice Stuffers

An invoice stuffer is a logical place for communication. Companies who bill their customers and don't take advantage of the opportunity to communicate are missing the boat. Because they are brief and included in the bill, invoice stuffers usually don't add to the mailing cost. The stuffer may just be a personal tips column, an announcement of a new service, or a discount offer. It should be designed to fit into the envelope in which the invoice is mailed.

Circulars

Circulars are multipage documents, often inserted in newspapers to announce sales. They may contain coupons and are usually printed on newsprint.

Calendar Listings

Most organizations have a monthly calendar of events. It is often the public relations person's task to collect that information and make it available in a format— and in time—to be useful to the reader.

The myriad details of *who, what, where, when,* and *why* must be included for each event. This can be a difficult task if organizations don't plan their activities well ahead of time. Calendar listings often appear in a newsletter and on posters for bulletin boards. A lively "Gee, I'd like to do that too" style of writing is required. Remember that you are selling the activity, not just listing it. If the calendar is also to be sent to the media, follow the suggested press-release format.

Letters

Letters from management to employees, from leaders to volunteers, from politicians to taxpayers, and for countless other purposes are often written by you, the communications professional. Letters to the editor are among the easiest placements to make. Just be sure that the letter is well written and organized, factual, and objective in tone. Letters to the editor tend to get read more often than a lengthy article, and they offer you or your organization a chance to be viewed as resources in a given field. Even if you write the letter, for greater impact it probably should be signed by your organization's management.

Feature Articles

Feature articles, when attributed to an officer of a company or organization, are called bylined expertise articles and are placed in the trade press. If the article is about marketing ideas, sign the marketing manager's name. If it concerns employee relations, sign the personnel person's name. A new product introduction would be bylined by the product manager. The editor of the trade magazine knows the person who signed the article is probably not the author of the piece, but that doesn't matter—just so you had approval.

Case Histories

Case histories are articles describing a customer application for your product or service—a "how they did it." Promotion takes a backseat to image building.

Approach the writing assignment by describing a problem that needed to be solved. Then talk about your person, product, or service and how it came to the rescue. Use lots of quotes for increased reader interest. Case histories are usually four to ten pages long, depending on the publication.

Case histories are easy to place in the trade press because they are not viewed as overtly sales-oriented, but they do provide the credibility that comes from first-person expression. Photographs, preferably location shots, should accompany the article.

Press Kits

A press kit, or press package, includes *all* the material you want to present about your product, person, or service.

The kit is usually a folder with inside pockets to hold the information. To personalize a press kit for a specific trade show or another purpose, have inexpensive custom-made stickers designed for the cover.

The content of the press kit includes:

- A short release about the new product or service being announced
- A background release about the company or technology being announced
- A fact sheet of important milestones or accomplishments in the field, or one with data on the product or service being announced
- Reprints of any good press you may have already received
- A capabilities brochure, if available
- Black-and-white photography and color slides for illustration and interest, with photo captions

The kit should contain enough information to be complete, but not so much that the reader/reporter will be turned off by the sheer volume of material.

Advertorials

Advertorials are a form of image advertising that was pioneered by Mobil Corporation's public relations department and now are seen regularly in major news magazines. Basically, advertorials combine an advertising medium (often a full page purchased in a magazine such as *Newsweek*) with a public relations message (such as "our company is a good and responsible corporate citizen"). Because this kind of image piece is extremely expensive, it is used mainly by large companies in conjunction with established advertising and public relations programs.

Public Service Announcements: Nonprofits' Alternative

Public service announcements (PSAs) are aired by radio and television stations free of charge as a community service. Only nonprofit organizations and government agencies can place PSAs, however; everyone else must buy advertising time.

The message conveyed must be noncommercial, nondenominational, politically nonpartisan, and not designed to influence legislation. Broadcast stations are restricted by law from airing information about lotteries, even if they are fund-raising events for nonprofit organizations.

Stations are not required to devote a fixed amount of time to nonprofit organizations, or to grant them any time at all. But stations pride themselves on being alert to community needs and are generally happy to help local nonprofits.

Every television and radio station has a person whose responsibility is community service. It's to your benefit to spend some time with each of these specialists. They can give you valuable tips on how to get air time, as well as specific guidelines for PSAs. They can also help you with the nitty-gritty of producing your own PSAs, often with the assistance of station on-air talent, using their equipment.

PSAs may be 10-, 20-, 30-, or 60-second spots and almost by definition are direct, focused, and concise. Count the number of words: on average, 25 words, 10 seconds; 50 words, 20 seconds; 65 words, 30 seconds; 150 words, about a minute. Give the time of the PSA on the script.

Write the copy to be spoken, not scanned by the eye. Be informal, but not breezy. Avoid adjectives and passive constructions, and be sure to give the essential facts of *who, what, when, where, why,* and *how.*

Give specific starting and ending dates for an event. The correct phrasing is "Monday, October 26, through Friday, October 30 . . . rather than "Monday through Friday."

If the copy contains difficult names or pronunciations, spell them phonetically.

As with news releases, type the script on one side of $8\frac{1}{2} \times 11$-inch paper, double spaced, and clearly state all pertinent information about your organization and the names of your contact persons.

VIDEOTAPE NEWS RELEASES ●

PR's New Wrinkle

You will have more success with the electronic media if you put your press releases in a format they understand—videotape. Videotape news releases (VNRs) are not inexpensive to produce, but they tend to get you airtime in this age of the saturated press.

The basic VNR formats are:

1. A complete script in print and on tape
2. A video release with a live reporter
3. A silent video release (which allows stations to provide voice)
4. A local contact name or source to target each video
5. A B-roll (background footage)

The primary method of distribution is often via satellite, with the video production house alerting the stations to the feed time. The buzzwords "uplink" and "downlink" describe the operation of making programming available and having the stations beam the program in at a certain, specified time when the satellite is distributing the information.

Big-city channels may be reluctant to use VNRs, but for not too much money you can have your videotape release aired on dedicated channels, called "industry television," that address such issues as health, finance, business, engineering, law, banking, insurance, cars, food, and accounting. Airtime is also available for sale on certain airlines just before the movies. And there is the Popcorn Report, which gives airtime of public relations items to be shown in theaters before the feature.

Just as it is difficult to find every placement you made for an idea or product, it is even more difficult to determine which television stations may have used your VNRs. Sometimes producers aren't even sure where the videotape they used came from. When relevant for background, VNRs are used, but you can't count on the television station to credit your company or to include any footage in which your company logo is clearly visible. For a better return on investment, plan on using the VNR you produce at a trade show or for company outreach if you arrange to be interviewed on a local television channel.

Credibility will increase the air play. High-quality footage of your product or service in action, interesting manufacturing operations, and brief corporate/management positioning statements should be available, "in the can," just in case you, your company, or organization needs to have its position stated clearly in the electronic press.

Anticipate spending about $30,000 on a simple release and distribution by satellite to about a hundred stations. Talk to more than one video production house to get competitive prices. Review other electronic public relations materials, including VNRs, and ask the video production house lots of questions about the placement ratio. You need results and accountability to support budgets of this magnitude.

5

A Quick Course in Good PR Writing

Writing: the activity we love to hate the most. Writers overeat and undersleep to avoid doing it. *Writer's Digest* says: "Writing is slow, tedious, agonizingly difficult work for 90 percent of all writers. The other 10 percent are no doubt lying."

Philip Lesly, an internationally known public relations expert, has this to say about writers: "The difference between a merely competent writer and a really good writer is the difference between a hamburger chef at McDonald's and the head chef at Lutèce: Both will provide you with sustenance, but only one will make a memorable impression on you."

The public relations writer must have two basic skills—versatility and creativity. Public relations people write a variety of pieces, often in the same day. Different situations call for different approaches to the same subject. Press releases sent to newspapers may be substantially different from those sent to radio stations. And the company newsletter will be written in a style that is not appropriate for the president's speech to the local Chamber of Commerce.

This need for versatility and creativity means that there is no magic formula for writing public relations materials. We would never capture a reader's or editor's interest if our writing were the same as everyone else's. Each piece of public relations writing—whether news release, newsletter, brochure, report, or other product—should be fresh and interesting.

Good writing incorporates eight elements: clarity, simplicity, brevity, vigor, precision, purpose, organization, and the human voice. Above all, it should attract the reader and make him or her want to keep reading.

Clarity

The primary objective of public relations writing is to convey information and ideas. To communicate effectively, the words and symbols you use must mean the same thing to the reader that they do to you. Your writing must be clear, understandable, and easy to read.

A careful writer will ask these questions about every sentence: What am I trying to say? What are the best words to express my message? What can I do to make it clearer? Have I gotten my message across?

Clear writers prefer the direct word to the fancy. Note that in nearly all of the following examples, the direct, familiar word is also the shorter one.

Fancy	Direct
accommodations	rooms
ameliorate	improve
commence	begin
remuneration	pay
deactivate	close, shut off
prior to	before
utilize	use
edifice	building
numerous	many
facilitate	ease
remainder	rest
implement	do, use
attempt	try
purchase	buy

Avoid words that add bulk but do nothing to enhance meaning. Some common redundancies:

Redundant	Direct
postpone until later	postpone
other alternative	alternative
first established	established
early pioneer	pioneer

Redundant	*Direct*
mixed together	mixed
revert back	revert

Work to make your writing crisper and stronger. Be especially alert to unnecessary modifiers, or intensifiers, such as "very" and "really." Are they (really) necessary?

Avoid the passive voice. As an example, here is the preceding sentence in the passive voice: "The passive voice is to be avoided." Such writing is weak, indirect, and wordy.

Use concrete words and phrases, rather than abstractions or jargon. Compare, for example, these two sentences:

> "At this present time we are experiencing precipitation."
> "The procedure will cause no physical discomfort."

. . . with these sentences:

> "It is raining."
> "It won't hurt."

The first examples use more and longer words, and some people might think they sound more sophisticated or educated. But they don't communicate as well as do the short, simple, direct statements of the second examples.

Simplicity

Which brings us to simplicity, the next element of good writing. "Good writing consists of the richest thoughts put into the simplest language," says Philip Lesly. The English language is indeed rich. An unabridged English dictionary contains more than 600,000 words, plus another 150,000 technical terms. But our spoken communications generally use fewer than 2,000 words. And, while most of us know some 20,000 words, the average working vocabulary includes only 600 to 1,000 words.

The most frequently used English words tend to be the shortest. According to some experts, the ten most-used words in the English language are: *the, of, and, a, to, in, is, you, that,* and *it*. The average length of these words is 2.4 letters; only "that" has more than three letters. A word coming into common use is often shortened: automobile becomes auto or car, television becomes TV, telephone becomes phone.

Good writers don't try to buck this trend; they go with it, using words that ordinary people use and understand. Newspaper editors won't think you're writing down to them when you send simply written releases—after all, the average American newspaper is written on a ninth-grade reading level.

Some writers, though, like to show off, which has led to some pretty tortuous stuff over the years. George

Orwell wrote the following to illustrate what he considered modern writing at its worst:

> Objective consideration of contemporary phenomena compel the conclusion that success or failure in competitive activities exhibits no tendency to be commensurate with innate capacity, but that a considerable element of the unpredictable must invariably be taken into account.

Does that make much sense? If you're a normal reader, you found the passage to be tedious, difficult to read or understand. Here's the same passage as Orwell originally found it:

> I returned and saw under the sun, that the race is not to the swift, nor the battle to the strong, neither yet bread to the wise, nor yet riches to men of understanding, nor yet favor to men of skill; but time and chance happeneth to them all.

Of the forty-nine words in the biblical version, only one has four syllables (*understanding*) and one has three syllables (*happeneth*). Forty-one of the remaining words have only one syllable. That's the way the paragraph originally happeneth.

The key to simple writing is simple language. And simple language, as the above example illustrates, doesn't have to talk down to the reader.

Brevity

Remember the old saying "Brevity is the soul of wit"? It's true of good writing, too. Brevity doesn't mean just length, although length is certainly part of the equation. It also means conciseness. An article, press release, speech, or announcement should be no longer than necessary to convey the message.

Abraham Lincoln had a pithy answer to the question "How long should a man's legs be?" that applies equally well to writing: "A man's legs should be long enough to reach the ground."

Short headlines, lead sentences, paragraphs, and articles are more effective than long ones. Some writers believe a "big" story deserves a "big" introduction. The opposite is usually true. Here's a classic example of a lead that's a model of brevity: "The President was shot in a theater tonight and perhaps mortally wounded." It was written, of course, on April 14, 1865, about Abraham Lincoln.

Vigor

Good writing is strong writing. Frank Grazian, editor of a respected newsletter for the communications industry, once wrote: "If you want to improve your writing, check your verbs first. They provide the key to making prose vigorous. In fact, you can usually vitalize any piece of writing by deleting verbs that slow down the pace of a sentence and substituting those that bring sentences to life."

Don't be afraid to put verbs to work. Many writers modify verbs with adjectives and nouns, usually weakening the verb as well as lengthening the sentence. Sometimes modifiers are necessary, but often they are merely indications of weak, unfocused, timid writing.

Weak/wordy	Strong/brief
held a meeting	met
put in an appearance	appeared
reached an agreement	agreed
taken into consideration	considered
submitted her resignation	resigned

Watch for long sentences that should be separated into two or more shorter sentences. A clue is a sentence that is full of clauses and phrases. A rule of thumb to help keep sentences short and vigorous: Avoid using more than two commas in a sentence.

Precision

As Mark Twain noted, "The difference between the right word and the almost right word is the difference between lightning and the lightning bug."

Say what you mean. Choose words carefully. Although we use very few of the words available to us in the English language, the ones we do use often have several meanings. Take the three-letter word "bar." Depending on the context in which it is used, it can mean:

• A place to buy liquor
• A device for prying
• An organization of lawyers
• A piece of gold or silver
• An obstacle
• A piece of soap or candy
• A sand formation

Be sure the meaning of the words you use fits the context and the intended audience.

Sentences with too many pronouns can be confusing, and it's good practice to keep a pronoun adjacent to the noun to which it refers. Here's an example of a sentence made imprecise by an unclear pronoun: "The president and vice president agreed that he would deliver the after-dinner speech."

Who will give the speech? The sentence doesn't tell you.

Imprecision also results from using jargon—words that are meaningless out of your profession or field of work. Each industry or group has its own language: lawyers, doctors, engineers, educators, hunters, farmers, even public relations people. Make sure the jargon of your profession doesn't creep into the materials you write for a general readership. Every word of every article should be clear to every intended reader.

Purpose

Public relations writers have a goal: to communicate a specific idea or set of facts. It's *not* to create beautiful phrases. Whenever you sit down to write, be it a simple press release or an elaborate brochure, think about why you're writing, who you're writing for, and what you want from your readers.

Depending on the piece, you may want to persuade, inform, influence, or educate your audience, or perhaps some combination of these goals. Whatever the goal, think it through before you begin writing. You'll find the result is tight, focused writing that is more persuasive, informative, and influential than copy written without a well-defined purpose.

Organization

Good writing is well organized. It takes the reader through the story or article in an orderly, logical manner. At the end, the reader knows *what* he or she has read—and, just as important, *why*.

While some writers believe that an outline is the only route to well-organized copy, others do equally well without a written outline. The effective writer, whether

THE INVERTED PYRAMID

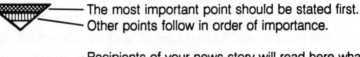 The most important point should be stated first.
Other points follow in order of importance.

Recipients of your news story will read here what,
who, where, when, and why.
Some readers will continue reading to get some
general background.
A few will want to read all the detail.

You may continue to use the inverted pyramid throughout the story. Each paragraph of the story may be constructed in inverted pyramid form.

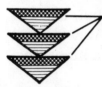 Begin each paragraph with a summary sentence, followed by subordinate detail. Link it to the next paragraph or group of facts summarized at the opening and elaborated in the lower part of the next triangle.

using an outline or not, knows that an article must flow easily and logically from one statement to another.

If you're having problems organizing a longer article for your newsletter, annual report, or brochure copy, try using the pyramid structure. This format—in which information is presented in descending order, from most important to least important—works well for many public relations communications. It is especially helpful for those new to public relations writing.

Quotable Quotes

Public relations materials are written by people for people. But sometimes the people get left out, and the result is dry, nonhuman writing. The best way to inject humanity into your writing is to include a human being, and that means quotations.

Quotation marks signal that a human voice is in residence. Unfortunately, many quotes sound like they were spoken by machines, not people. That's because all too often the poor public relations person is required to make up quotes for people who are too busy to think of what they'd like to say themselves. Quotations should add to the story, not repeat something that's already there.

If you do find yourself having to write a quote, read it out loud before you include it. Or say it to someone else. Does it sound like a real person talking, or is it "officialese"? If you know the person you're writing the quote for, think about how he or she speaks. Any catch phrases that sum up the person's style? Don't be afraid to sound too human. Experience shows that the only way you can go wrong is if you use substandard English.

With each quotation you'll use a phrase, beginning with a verb such as "said," to identify the speaker. This verb is called an attributive verb. "Said" is not the only attributive verb to use, but it is often the best. The reader's eye skims over it, as this example shows:

> "The word 'said' is short, clear, neutral, accurate, and best of all, invisible," said the writer.

Other attributive words that are acceptable are "continued" and "added." Attributive verbs to avoid include: stated, declared, snapped, asserted, smiled, wept, proclaimed, avowed, laughed, cautioned, insisted, and predicted. Though many journalists avoid using "pointed out" or "noted," public relations writers often use them to give the speaker an authoritative tone.

Books Every Writer Should Have

There are many books on writing, and each has something to offer. We believe the following books are essential for people who care about good writing.

The Elements of Style, by William Strunk, Jr., and E. B. White (Macmillan), is the best known and most respected handbook for writers. It gives excellent suggestions for improving your writing style.

The Associated Press Stylebook, published by The Associated Press, serves as a guide to generally accepted journalistic practices, such as the proper abbreviations for states' names, or when to spell out numbers and when to use numerals. It also functions as a dictionary of commonly misspelled words.

On Writing Well, by William Zinsser (Harper & Row), is not a reference book on specific usage. It is, however, an indispensible guide, written in a graceful, witty, and authoritative style.

The Synonym Finder, by J. I. Rodale (Warner Books), is a new-style thesaurus. Organized alphabetically, the book does away with the tedious hunt-and-seek method that Roget's thesaurus required. It incorporates a generous helping of modern synonyms, as well as the older terms that abound in Roget's.

Last, any good dictionary. We're not going to make a specific recommendation since there are so many available and so many opinions on which is best. We each own several, and so do all the other writers we know. Just make sure to keep one close at hand and use it often. It won't just help your spelling; you'll find that regular use of a good dictionary will strengthen your writing as well.

6

What To Get and How To Get It: Nailing Down the Facts

Chapter 5 covered the basics of good writing and the mechanics of writing for public relations in particular. This chapter will cover two areas of prime importance to public relations writers: what to write about and how to interview sources.

What to Write About, or "No News Is Bad News"

The adage "no news is good news" may be true in some situations, but the idea of no news at all is the stuff of nightmares for public relations writers.

A dearth of news is a prime opportunity for the public relations staff to put on their journalists' hats and go hunting for a story. Probably several good ones are just waiting to be discovered. Some of the best stories lie hidden in back offices, where people are quietly going about their jobs.

To help you get started, here is a list of fifty common public relations stories, grouped by category. We've provided a simple key to identify which story ideas are geared for internal audiences and therefore for internal publications, such as employee newsletters (the letter "I" follows those suggestions), and which ideas are geared to external, general audiences (the letter "E" follows those suggestions). Some, as you'll see, are appropriate for both.

Stories About Employees

Employees are an incredibly rich source of stories, especially goodwill stories that stress the human aspect of the company or organization. Collect ideas for employee stories assiduously; if you have a good file on hand, you'll never be at a loss when you find yourself just one story short for this month's newsletter.

1. Profile an interesting employee: someone who's different; someone who has overcome great obstacles to get where he or she is today; someone who's been with the company for a long time and can reflect on changes.   I

I = Internal publications

2. Report on promotions.   I

3. Report on job changes.   I

4. Announce the hiring of new employees or staff. "So-and-so has joined XYZ Company" stories abound. While they may seem boring to you, the lists of new appointments in the business pages are among the first items that readers turn to.   I, E

5. Let the world know your employees and staff members are involved in their professions. Give them credit for their extracurricular activities. Report employee and staff attendance at conventions and professional conferences, including professional development classes.   I, E

6. Announce speeches given by employees.   I

7. Report on the content of employees' speeches. I

8. Announce or feature retirements. This is your last chance to thank someone for years of service, and to get the retiree and your organization a little publicity in the bargain.   I, E

9. Announce awards given by professional organizations.   I, E

10. Report on unusual hobbies of staff and employees.   I

11. Report on employee and staff participation in civic and community groups.   I

I = Internal publications
E = External publications

12. Announce employee or staff appointments to boards of directors or other positions of responsibility in the community.   **I, E**

13. Report on employee group activities: tours, trips, etc.   **I**

Stories About VIPs

A board of directors or trustees can be a good source of stories, as can the organization's relationship with community leaders.

1. Introduce new directors. ("New" is a relative term here; anyone who joined the board in the past year can be counted as new.)   **I, E**

2. Write about retiring directors.   **I**

3. Announce directors named to offices (chairman, etc.) or to board committees.   **I, E**

4. Announce visits to the company by public or industry leaders or recognized members of a profession.   **I**

5. Report on VIP visits.   **I**

6. Profile a visitor. This can be done either before or after the visit. Before, it serves as a good introduction to the person; afterwards, it can tell those who didn't get to meet the visitor what he or she is like.   **I**

I = Internal publications
E = External publications

Stories About the Company or Organization

1. Announce new company or organizational policies.   I

2. Publicize new policies that will have a direct effect on the public, or those that might be of interest to the public and that would also enhance the company or organizational image.   E

3. Publicize milestones in production or services. Someone should be keeping track of how many widgets have been made or how many clients were served. Tell the world when you hit a significant number (or even a nice round number).   I, E

4. Profile the company or organization on its anniversary. When was it founded? Why? How has it changed since then? People have a fascination with comparing where we've been to where we are now.   I, E

5. Profile the company or organization founder(s)—a terrific way to tie in to an anniversary celebration.   I

6. Announce minority programs.   I, E

7. Update the community on your minority programs. How have they progressed? What successes can you report?   E

8. Announce open houses for families, friends, and the community. If you have an open house that's not open to the public, report on it afterwards.   I, E

I = Internal publications
E = External publications

9. Publicize participation in charitable events and organizations. This includes corporate donations of time or equipment, as well as money.   I, E

10. Announce corporate gifts to organizations.   E

11. Announce contests sponsored by the company. Again, if it is a purely internal affair (an employee raffle, for example), report on the outcome.   I, E

12. Announce participation in parades and other community events.   I

13. Notify the public of the annual meeting and then report on the meeting.   E

14. Profile an attendee at the annual meeting. Did a 12-year-old investor attend? How about a 92-year-old? Is there someone who's been at every meeting since 1943 (but owns only five shares of stock)?   E

15. Announce growth—new facilities, new acquisitions, staff expansions.   I, E

16. Announce equipment or facility improvements— new computer systems, for example—that enhance the functioning of the company or organization.   I, E

17. Report on the success (and defeats) of athletic teams sponsored by the company or organization. Profile the team members.   I

18. Release quarterly statements with explanations.   I, E

19. Release the annual report with explanations.   I, E

I = Internal publications
E = External publications

Stories About Products or Programs

1. Release information on new products, programs, or services.   E

2. Release information on improved products or expanded programs.   E

3. Announce discontinued products or programs—with an explanation. This can make a good news story; for example, a nonprofit program that ended because it was successful and solved a problem.   E

4. Announce price changes.   E

5. Profile new or unusual product applications. What are customers doing with the product? Is it something unexpected, something new?   E

6. Announce availability of a new brochure (also known as a literature release).   E

7. Interpret news events that have an effect on your company, industry, or organization.   E

Stories About Buildings or Facilities

1. Announce and report on new-building dedications.   I, E

2. Profile the move to a new facility. Are there interesting/amusing "horror" stories from the move? Was the move handled in an unusual way? (If you're planning a caravan of 100 cars from one building to another

I = Internal publications
E = External publications

with employees and staff carrying their belongings, you can generate a terrific goodwill story in the media.) This is especially good for large companies that are perceived as faceless. **I, E**

3. Announce new facility plans and release a picture of the architect's rendering. These illustrations get a surprising amount of play on the business pages, where the editors are generally desperate for a good photo. **I, E**

4. Announce and report on cornerstone-laying ceremonies and time capsules. And put a "tickler" (reminder) in a file so you (or a successor) remember to do a story when it's time to open the capsule. An amazing number of time capsules are forgotten and never opened. **I, E**

5. Publicize your building's amenities. Feature stories can highlight the cafeteria (where top management and maintenance staff eat side by side), an art exhibit in the lobby, or the interior design of office suites. **I, E**

When All Else Fails . . .

The well is dry. You've looked, but there are absolutely no stories out there. You have nothing to talk about. The company hasn't introduced a new product in ages,

---

I = Internal publications
E = External publications

the quarterly report won't come out for another month, and employees are beginning to avoid you in the halls.

Consider creating a reason for news. No, not *creating* news, but creating a *reason* for it. How? Through "tie-ins." Use something outside your company that is newsworthy, something that already has the public's attention (or at least the media's) and tie your story to it. Here are a few samples:

TIE-INS TO SPECIFIC DATES. There are all sorts of dates that a company finds fascinating: the founder's birthday, the anniversary of the move to the "new" building, the anniversary of the introduction of your most successful product or service.

TIE-INS TO "NAME" DATES. If you don't have any special dates on your own corporate or organizational calendar to highlight, check *Chase's Annual Events,* compiled by William D. and Helen M. Chase. This guide is updated annually and lists such events as National Pickle Month, Better Hearing Month, National Better Spelling Week, and other events that you can write a story about. A dentist, for example, might want some publicity when National Smile Day comes around.

TIE-INS TO NATIONAL HOLIDAYS. Department stores do it. Why shouldn't you?

TIE-INS TO NATIONAL ISSUES. A political campaign year is the perfect tie-in for the small local company that makes lapel pins. It's even better if the company is asked to make both donkey and elephant pins. Or, a community organization could make good copy on a campaign issue.

TIE-INS TO LOCAL NEWS. A regional drought is a good time to publicize your company's water-saving efforts. It could also be a chance for you to place a light human-interest story on the bottled water your company provides for employees in the media. A nonprofit organization would also have plenty of stories that link with local events.

EVEN BAD NEWS. Problems—even catastrophes—on the national level can sometimes be turned into good news locally. A major drought that cripples farmers nation-wide might well keep people away from the local farmer's market. This might be a good time for a release on how the farmer's market has grown beyond the traditional fruits and vegetables to include many other items for the home and family.

Interview Techniques and Fact Gathering

You've decided on a story. Now what? The success of any article you write depends on the depth and accuracy of the information gathered and communicated. Day after day, the public relations person is faced with the task of making fresh what is routine, or becoming an instant expert on complicated subjects.

Obviously, expertise takes more than the forty-five minutes you've devoted to reading through a file or magazine article you managed to dig up in the library. In addition to research, then, public relations people need to interview experts, and they must exhibit the same interviewing skills as a seasoned reporter.

Set Your Objectives

Before you call the person you want to interview, determine why the interview is necessary. What specific information do you need? Is this the right person to turn to for that information? You should know the publication you intend the article to appear in and the approximate length of the finished piece. Will it be bylined by the interviewee, or will the interviewee serve as a resource only? Will the person be quoted directly or used only as a source of background information? Put the objectives in writing to force yourself to think out the article thoroughly.

Do as much research as possible before the interview. Then, using the information you have gathered, develop a written list of pertinent questions. Make sure the questions lead in some meaningful direction. Learn one or two catch phrases, or buzzwords, from that person's specialty. Write down the items you need from the interviewee: copies of articles, photographs, samples of his or her work—whatever you think you might need.

Set the Stage

The person you want to interview might be from the office next door or from a company in the next city, but your behavior and demeanor should be consistent and professional regardless of whom you contact. We will assume here that you want to interview someone based out of town; just skip the steps that are unnecessary when doing in-town (or in-house) interviews.

A telephone call works best when setting up an appointment for an interview, but if you can't reach the person or someone is screening calls (and screening you out), write a letter. This initial contact will set the tone for the eventual meeting, so introduce yourself, state your reasons for calling or writing, and mention the person who recommended him or her, if appropriate. Tell the person exactly how much time you think you'll need and then stick to it, unless he or she agrees to more time.

This is a good time for "strokes," or a brief explanation of why that person is critical to the success of your article or project. People are often flattered when asked for an interview. Suddenly, "plain old me" becomes an expert and a writer wants an interview. Play on this feeling. The person then has a stake in seeing the finished piece in print.

Finally, mention if you intend to use a tape recorder. Your goal is to make the interviewee as comfortable as possible, and that includes preventing any unwelcome surprises from popping up the day of the interview.

To be completely professional and make a great impression, follow up the telephone conversation with a letter confirming the time, date, place, and subject matter of the interview. This will also prevent your arriving on the second day of the month and discovering that the person didn't expect you until the twenty-second.

Use Proven Question-and-Answer Techniques

The interview is about to begin. The best way to start may be to offer your business card and request the interviewee's. This gives each of you a reliable record of names, titles, and company or organization. Then, after a brief introduction (including your appreciation for the person's time and expertise and a quick review of your own credentials), you may want to preview the topics you plan to cover.

Don't be afraid to ask the person to speak more slowly or to repeat or explain something you didn't understand. If the answers don't seem specific enough, try leading with a question such as "Could you elaborate on that?" Don't let the person assume that you know anything. Have him or her explain things thoroughly if you don't understand.

Even if the person seems incapable of finishing sentences and seemingly wants you to pipe in and add something, don't do it. If you plan to quote the person directly, you'll need it in his or her words, not yours. A common mistake inexperienced interviewers make is to assume something without confirming it, and then having to go back for the correction (which can be time-consuming, costly, unprofessional, and sometimes embarrassing).

Even if you use a tape recorder, take adequate notes. Recorders have undone a United States president, and they can work against you, too. Make sure the batteries are fresh and that you are familiar with the equipment. And don't count on a borrowed recorder at the last minute, ever.

Before ending the interview, ask if you have left anything out or if there is something the person would like to add. Don't close your notebook as you ask the question. This can be a nearly magic moment, when the person being interviewed unwinds and gives you the best quote of the day, or when he or she comes up with something you never even thought of that changes the entire story.

Pay attention to the time and don't overstay your welcome—unless, of course, the subject is obviously enjoying the interview and it would seem rude to leave. Set the stage for a possible follow-up by phone in case you do find yourself in need of more facts. Simply explain that once you begin to write you may find some information missing. Just as you began on a conversational note, try to conclude with something light and friendly, and promise whatever is appropriate for approvals and follow-up.

A word of caution. People will promise to send you more information, and mean it, but very few will remember once you leave the room. So before you leave, make copies of any information you can't take with you. If the person you have interviewed has some information back in the office, walk with him or her and get it. You can never have too much background material when the time comes to write up the interview.

The Nine Commandments of Interviewing

- Be on time, and leave on time.
- Never argue.
- Show enthusiasm and be curious about the subject at hand.
- Avoid making jokes or expressing strong opinions.
- Bring an ample supply of paper and writing tools.
- Ask for permission before turning on the tape recorder.
- Stick to the point—don't get sidetracked by chitchat.
- Return promptly and in good condition all materials on loan to you.
- Remember that interviewing is a skill that improves with experience.

Interview Preparation

Ask if any of the background materials you want are available, such as a history of the company or any articles the person may have written. This will give him or her time to gather them for you and have them ready at the interview. You also may want to refer to some of the questions you intend to ask. And if a photograph will be taken, be sure to mention that fact. Lots of people are camera-shy and won't enjoy being taken by surprise.

Discuss the approvals process. People will often speak more freely if they are assured they will have a chance to look over the article before it is published. While it is rare for a practicing journalist to agree to prior approval, it is extremely common in public relations.

Choose a day and time that is convenient to your subject. If the interview is to be at his or her office, suggest using a conference room, where phone calls and visitors will not interrupt the process. Be sure to do this before you arrive for the interview because many companies and organizations require employees to reserve conference rooms in advance.

Don't overlook the obvious. Ask for directions and learn if parking could be a problem. (Imagine a scenario that puts you out on the street, looking for a parking spot, while the president of a large company waits for you. Not a pretty sight.)

The best time to work on writing up the interview is right after you conduct it. You're still interested in the subject, your notes still make sense, and the personality of the interviewee is still fresh in your mind. At least organize your notes so that the relevant points will become apparent, and jot down some of your impressions.

7

Working with the Media

The term "the media" incorporates a large, loose-knit group of newspeople working in a variety of communications: print, wire services, radio, television, and other video productions. Within those groups are subgroupings: local, regional, national, special interest, and trade. Local media include all those that work in and cover your city or town. Regional media are those in a wider geographic area, such as upstate New York or southern California. The national media include network television and radio programs, news magazines, such as *Time* and *Newsweek,* and the major wire services, including The Associated Press (AP) and UPI. A handful of newspapers are also considered national publications: *The New York Times, The Los Angeles Times, The Washington Post, The Philadelphia Inquirer, The Chicago Sun-Times,* and, of course, *USA Today.*

The Wall Street Journal is often included in this classification, although some consider it a business publication. That would put it in the special-interest category, along with the phenomenally successful women's magazines and publications affiliated with such organizations as the National Rifle Association and the American Association of Retired Persons (whose magazine, *Modern Maturity,* has one of the highest circulations in the country).

The last media category, trade, consists of magazines and news shows geared toward specific professions, such as lawyers, plumbers, engineers, and writers. There are literally hundreds of trade publications, some published as often as weekly, most monthly or quarterly.

What all of these news outlets have in common is an insatiable need for information. The more often a magazine is published or a show is aired, the greater its need. Daily newspapers, for instance, must fill hundreds of inches of column space with relevant, up-to-date articles. It is impossible for them to go out and gather this information alone. Their resources are too limited, and deadlines too tight and too often. New material is needed every day of the week.

What Do the Media Want from You?

The answer is simple: information. Instead of hiring hundreds of reporters, newspapers and other media outlets turn to public relations materials, which conveniently tell them everything they need to know about the many events and stories in the community each week—*who* is doing *what, where, when,* and *why,* the five W's a journalist lives by.

You, the public relations person, can provide this information in a number of ways, depending on the situation and the news person's needs (as well as your objectives). This information comes in an array of prepared editorial materials:

- Press kits (which can include several of the elements listed below)
- News releases
- Calendar listings
- How-to articles
- Photographs
- Background releases (also called backgrounders)
- Fact sheets
- Exclusive articles
- Case histories (also called case studies)
- Query letters

You might choose to use materials that already exist, such as product literature, newsletters, brochures, and technical data, in addition to those items listed above, which are developed strictly for the media. Other ways to disseminate information to the media include in-person and telephone interviews, press conferences, and tours of your facilities.

Inside the Media: How They Operate

INDEPENDENT OF ADVERTISING. In principle, the editorial staff is separate from the advertising side of the business. They usually don't know and don't care if your company is a big advertiser. Don't try to use your ads as a reason to be (or not be) covered. It probably won't work. Mobil Corporation pulled all of its advertising from *The Wall Street Journal* several years ago because the company was angry about negative coverage it had received. The paper is still going strong without Mobil's advertising, and it still covers the company extensively.

PHOTOS. Newspapers seldom use photographs from public relations sources, but trade magazines are always eager for good photos. The exception in daily newspapers is the business section. Editors try to have at least one photo on the front page of the section, and they look for ones that are eye-catching.

INVIOLATE DEADLINES. A deadline is a deadline is a deadline. No excuses accepted. Ever.

STAFF-WRITTEN ARTICLES. You'll seldom have a press release reproduced in its entirety in a daily newspaper, and almost never on television or radio. Reporters pride themselves on their independence and nonreliance on public relations people—never mind that they do rely on us a great deal. The exceptions to this rule are weekly newspapers, which tend to be under-staffed, and trade magazines.

LEAD TIMES. This is the amount of time between development of a story idea and when the story actually runs. For monthly magazines, this can be as long as six months; for a daily newspaper, as short as several hours. Knowing the average lead time for the media you work with will enable you to produce and distribute information on time. You can't send a monthly magazine a release in March and expect coverage in the April, or even May, issue. Lead time for local media (newspapers, television, and radio) is about one week.

TELEPHONE CALLS. Media people are busy and hardworking. They have neither the time nor patience for telephone conversations when they're on deadline, or to answer your trivial questions at any time of the day. ("Did you get my release?" is the most frequently asked—and most annoying—question reporters get. They'll say yes just to get rid of you, even though they have no idea whether yours is one of the hundreds piled on their desk at any given moment.)

The exception to the telephone rule is trade press editors. They will accept phone calls, even the did-you-get-it calls that other editors dislike. Try phrasing those questions differently, though. Ask if they have any questions about the information you sent, or if there is any more information you can provide for them. Would they like, for example, photography to illustrate the article?

Developing a Media List

- Determine *which* are the most appropriate news outlets and *who* is the most appropriate person to contact there.
- Find out *when* their deadlines are.
- Research *what* subjects they cover.
- Know *where* the geographic areas they cover begin and end.
- Determine *why* they should cover your story.
- Decide *how* you can best reach them.

To get started on creating the actual list, use the telephone book. Then use the telephone itself to flesh out the details. Exactly who should you contact with news about a manufacturing company? A hardware store? A child-care center? Switchboard operators should be able and willing to give you the name and title of the person to be contacted. Or ask for the assignment editor at television stations, the news director at radio stations, and the city editor at newspapers. These are all people who are in the know, and if they don't have the time to help you, they can pass you on to someone who does.

Nonprofit organizations have their own network to tap into—other nonprofits. Public relations practitioners in nonprofits are helpful about sharing information and pointers with each other. If you do get a media list from other practitioners, however, thank them extravagantly and then don't trust it. Verify all the information for yourself. Media people change jobs often, so call and ask if you have the right name before you send a letter to someone who left six months ago.

Some local chapters of professional organizations, such as the Public Relations Society of America and Women in Communications, Inc., publish media lists, as does the local library. Whatever the source of your list, check it carefully for yourself.

Media Reference Sources

Books and directories are available that list all the media outlets across the country. Some include names of editors and brief descriptions of the media outlets. Visit the library and look at as many as possible to get an idea of which will best serve your needs. Prices range from about $70 to nearly $400. Here is a sampling of what's available:

Bacon's Media Directories. PR and Media Information Systems, Chicago, IL. Three directories are available: Magazines, Newspapers, and Radio/TV. Bacon's also publishes an international directory.

Working Press of the Nation. National Research Bureau, Chicago IL. Five volumes are available: Newspapers, Magazines, TV and Radio Stations, Feature Writers and Photographers, and Internal Publications.

The Standard Periodical Directory. Oxbridge Communications, Inc., New York, NY. This one-volume directory gives extensive information on magazines.

All-In-One Directory. Gebbie Press, New Paltz, NY. Includes brief listings on magazines, newspapers, radio and television, and special-interest publications.

Editor and Publisher Yearbook. The Editor & Publisher Company, New York, NY. This monthly magazine publishes an annual yearbook issue that lists newspapers across the country.

Media Relations Dos and Don'ts

- *Do* get to know your news contacts.
- *Do* create a list of contacts for newspaper and magazine editors, as well as broadcast personnel. The list may include several people from each publication, because different stories may appeal to different editors.
- *Do* read the publication (or watch or listen to the broadcast) so you know what it covers and what its style is.
- *Do* check all of your news materials for accuracy before releasing them. All facts and figures should be

double checked. Remember that spelling and grammar count; proofread carefully.

- *Do* keep all your communications simple, accurate, and direct.
- *Do* adhere strictly to deadlines. Even if you have to hand-deliver materials to get them to a reporter by deadline, do it.
- *Do* answer calls from the media promptly. If you can't talk to them at that moment, ask when their deadline is and set a time for returning their call.
- *Do* invite newspeople to tour your organization's headquarters or the company's plant.
- *Do* have a specific purpose for every press release you send out. "For the sake of staying in touch with editors" is not a good enough reason. Each release must have news value.
- *Do* take no for an answer. Don't beg or plead. Just learn from the experience. Make a stronger case next time if you have to, or make a note that a particular editor isn't interested in certain kinds of stories.
- *Do* write thoughtful, literate query letters suggesting stories, and make sure the letters are brief and to the point.
- *Do* contact only one person at any given media outlet with a certain story. If you have a good reason to contact two people, let each know that.
- *Do* be creative. Fresh ideas and new angles are what the media are looking for.
- *Do* consider the visual aspect of stories you propose to television or for other video use.

- *Do* maintain ongoing contacts with important media representatives, even when you don't have a news item for them.
- *Do* be courteous and polite at all times.
- *Do* point out serious or embarrassing errors in a story, but be sure to do it nicely, politely, and helpfully.
- *Do* thank your contacts for their time and interest.
- *Don't* make friendly visits at deadline time.
- *Don't* deliver news stories to the advertising department.
- *Don't* try to influence coverage. Simply explain why your story is important to the community, and let the editor decide whether or not to use it.
- *Don't* depend on fluff. Emphasize the news value of your stories.
- *Don't* overpromise. If you just *hope* that the governor of the state will be at your ground-breaking ceremony, don't promise his attendance. And if he cancels at the last minute, let the media know he won't be there. You may not get coverage this time, but you'll get respect.
- *Don't* say anything you cannot prove. If you find yourself in need of a statistic, don't guess—look it up.
- *Don't* use such adjectives as "outstanding" or "wonderful," unless in quotes. Otherwise you will be inserting your opinion into a piece.
- *Don't* use the word "unique" unless you truly have a claim to uniqueness. Reporters are sick of hearing about identical unique programs and products.

- *Don't* let a good news story get old. Old news (meaning anything that happened before today) doesn't get covered.
- *Don't* answer any question with "no comment." It's rude and brusque. Instead, explain why you can't discuss a certain topic.
- *Don't* ask for a retraction or write a nasty letter or make an angry phone call when you disagree with the contents of a story; you'll be resented. Instead, cool off and decide rationally how you will correct any misinformation that appears in the press (and simply ignore minor errors).
- *Don't* ask to review a story before it is printed. Occasionally, a trade press editor will show you a story, but we advise not asking anyone for prior review. It indicates that you suspect that the reporter won't get the story right.
- *Don't* ask a reporter to take information over the telephone. If he or she calls *you* for a telephone interview, that's different. But don't expect a reporter to waste precious time on the telephone when you could have mailed the information.
- *Don't* ever talk "off the record." There is no such thing. If you don't want the reporter to write it, don't say it.

Special Needs of Television

Here are some tips for handling television broadcast interviews:

- Keep answers short. The typical sound bite, or quote from an interviewee in a news story, lasts from 10 to 15 seconds. That's all. If you ramble, the reporter will have a difficult time excerpting a useful quote.
- Arrive early for studio interviews. Become familiar with the set and the setting; the goal is to appear comfortable.
- Think of the camera or microphone as your audience. But do not look directly into the camera—look at your interviewer.
- Familiarize yourself in advance with the particular broadcast or talk show you will be on.
- Speak in your normal tone of voice.
- Dress conservatively. Men should wear dark, plain suits and pastel-colored or off-white shirts. Avoid bow ties or ties with busy patterns or wild colors. Stay away from checks, plaids, and small patterns. Women should wear solid colors and avoid outfits with frills or lace. Simple is best. Muted colors look better than white or light pastels. Keep jewelry to a minimum. If you will be shown on screen below the waist, men should wear dark socks that cover the calf; women should make sure that when they are seated their dresses do not rise too far above the knee.
- Men should shave before going on camera; women should wear conservative makeup.
- Speak slowly and calmly. The reporter may use a rapid-fire speaking pace. If you get caught up in the same rhythm, you could find yourself stumbling over your words.

- Pauses can be edited out at a later date. A pause that seemed to last for hours to you is in reality only one or two seconds long. Don't worry about it. Even on live interview shows, you'll seem more in control if you pause to think before jumping in with a reply.
- If you are seated during the interview, lean forward slightly. Don't sit back, and don't drape your arm over the back of the chair. You may feel better, but you will look less than professional. Also remember that the most graceful way for women to sit is with ankles crossed.
- Don't touch your face or play with your hair, glasses, or jewelry. Feel free to make a moderate amount of gestures with your hands, but don't wave them about. Women: If you habitually play with your necklace, don't wear one during the interview. Keep your hands loosely folded in your lap.

Press Conferences and Special Events

Press Conferences

Press conferences are media-specific events—that is, there is no other reason to get together except that the media will be there. If only two reporters turn up for your press conference, is it automatically a failure? When should you hold a press conference? The best advice we've ever heard is to hold press conferences either seldom or never!

The people who are most enamored of press conferences are boards of directors, trustees, or upper corporate management. These are the people who are most likely to be enchanted by your organization's or company's good news. Sales are up? Hold a press conference, says the corporate vice-president. The capital campaign is near its goal? Hold a press conference, and remind the public that we're still raising money, says the chairman of the board of directors.

In reality, the only good press conference is the one that takes place after the public relations person has determined that there is absolutely no other way to disseminate the information.

One valid reason to hold a press conference: a famous sports figure is visiting your company for the day to give a motivational speech. The press conference allows you to link your name to the sports figure's and lets the media, and through them the public, meet the celebrity. The fact that the speaker is famous in this example is no accident: An unknown motivational speaker, although terrific for your employees, will not draw the media.

If you do decide to hold a press conference, here are some tips for getting the most out of the event:

- Make sure the conference is newsworthy and that the media will attend. If you're not sure, call a few of your key contacts in the media and ask them if they'd come.

- Don't serve alcohol.
- Don't leak information that will be presented at the press conference to anyone in advance.
- Find one or two different angles to the story. Then, if you're lucky and several reporters want to follow up, you can provide each with a different idea.
- Have press kits available at the door, and be sure to have enough.
- Hand-deliver press kits to those who did not attend. Make sure you don't penalize the media outlets that didn't send someone.
- Have enough staff in attendance to keep the conference running smoothly.
- Schedule the conference for a time convenient to the media. Television stations, for instance, have difficulty covering anything before 10 A.M., and they can't stay past 4 P.M.—they need to rush back to the station to write and edit their stories.
- Hold the conference in an accessible, comfortable setting. If your organization or company's offices are difficult to find or far from the center of town, consider using a place that's easier to get to. Provide simple and explicit directions, including information on parking.
- Prepare as you would for any interview situation.

Special Events

Special events are luncheons, outings, meetings, or "happenings" to which you might want to invite the media. They are not organized with the media in mind, however, so if no reporters show up you still have a reason to assemble. Media coverage is often just an extra.

The tips for press conferences also hold true for handling the media at special events. It is especially important to make sure that you have enough people available to help any media who arrive. You might get tied up with a television news team, helping them find the right person to interview or showing them something of interest, so have someone available to do the same for the newspaper reporter and photographer who arrive five minutes later.

Let participants in the event know that there may—or may not—be media representatives at the event. Don't build it up or make it sound as if this is the most important part of the event. They'll only be disappointed when the television cameras don't show up.

The downside of events is that they are out of your control. Something may happen that you wish the media had never seen. You will have to handle these situations as best as you can. We've learned that honesty is the best policy.

Here is a real-life example of what can go wrong at an event and how the situation was handled: Two days before a ground-breaking ceremony for a nonprofit agency's new multimillion-dollar building, a union group notified the agency that it planned to picket the ceremony because it had a dispute with the contractor the agency had hired. Local dignitaries, including the mayor, had been invited and planned to attend, as did many media representatives.

The best plan of action was honesty. The mayor and the other dignitaries received phone calls alerting them to the possible presence of a picket line and offering them the choice of backing out. Most did. The media also were called and told of the expected pickets, and a press release that explained the situation and the agency's position was prepared and handed out at the event.

Three television stations, two daily newspapers (morning and afternoon), two weekly newspapers, and one radio station covered the event. The picketers received little or no media attention. Only one photograph appeared in print and none of the television stations showed any picketers. The result of the entire affair was good coverage for the agency and strengthened relationships with both the media and local VIPs.

THE MEDIA INTERVIEW ●

What to Do Before, During, and After

You've gotten a response to a press release—a reporter has called and wants to interview someone in your organization. You've identified the person and set a time and place, discussed any materials the reporter needs, and told both parties that you

QUICK CHECKLIST FOR PRESS CONFERENCES
AND SPECIAL EVENTS

- Type of meeting (breakfast, cocktails, coffee break, meeting only)
- Place (hotel, restaurant, club, office)
- Location
- Room arrangements (seating plan, head table, lectern)
- Organization of meals
- Invitations
- Program (agenda, speech writing, photographer, presentation materials)
- Equipment needed (presentation, tape recorder, public address system)
- Press materials (release, kits, photographs, press kit covers)
- Press activities (advance copies of release and/or speeches and roundup reports)

will be in attendance as well. The reporter is happy, but the interviewee is worried and has lots of questions for you: What's going to happen? What if there are questions about classified material, or information the organization doesn't want to make public? What if a question can't be answered?

Here is a checklist of steps that an interviewee (whether it's you or an expert in your company) should take to prepare for an interview. This is assuming ideal circumstances, of course.

There will be occasions when you don't have the luxury to spend time preparing—but you will probably always have time to take a quick look at this list, take a deep breath, and relax.

BEFORE THE INTERVIEW

Research the interviewer and the media outlet. Be prepared to answer the following questions for your expert:

- Name of magazine, newspaper, television or radio station?
- Topic of the story or article?
- Reporter's name? Background?
- How much does the reporter know about the subject?
- Areas to be covered during the interview?

Anticipate what the interview situation will be like:

- What specific questions will be asked? Brainstorm as many as possible.
- Might questions be asked that you don't want to answer?
- How will you handle these questions? Role-play with each other and practice answering tough questions.

Prepare for the interview as you would any speaking engagement:

- Have facts and figures organized and at hand (not buried in a stack of reports on your desk).
- Think about and write down the points you want to make.
- Determine the most important points.
- Rehearse—but don't memorize—answers to questions.

DURING THE INTERVIEW

Follow these five steps to giving a good interview:

1. Communicate the important points first.
2. State conclusions, then briefly explain how you reached them.

3. Answer questions and then bridge to another topic. "That reminds me of another important factor . . ." is an example of bridging.

4. Look for opportunities to make your point, even if the interviewer doesn't raise the subject.

5. Give the interviewer your business card, or write down your name and title.

Reporters use six basic types of questions:

1. *The straightforward question.* This deserves a straightforward response.

2. *The puff question.* This has little or no substance. It gives you a chance to lead the conversation to what you consider important.

3. *The hypothetical question.* "What if" questions are designed to lead you into conjecture. Do not fall into this trap. Politely but firmly refuse to talk about what might have been or what could be.

4. *The fact-filled question.* These "facts" may or may not be true. You have no way of knowing. Questions that ask you to comment on or respond to "a recent study" do not have to be answered if you are not familiar with the study. Ask for a copy of it and say you'll be happy to comment (if you believe you're qualified to do so) after reading it.

5. *The leading question.* This type of question starts with "Don't you think that . . . ?" Be wary of questions that could put words in your mouth. On the other hand, if you do indeed agree, say so and paraphrase the question in your response. The re-

porter may simply be looking for a good quote from you, so a yes or no answer will not be helpful.

6. *The multiple-part question.* Think of it as a multiple-choice question on a test. Politicians get these all the time. They choose the part(s) they like best and ignore the rest.

AFTER THE INTERVIEW

Follow up with the reporter. If you promised to provide further information, make sure you do so promptly and completely. Don't hesitate to let the reporter know if you liked the story—or, if you didn't, why not (courteously but specifically). Often your in-house expert will tell *you* how happy he or she was with the story; be sure to pass that along. Everyone likes to know their work is appreciated.

8

When Crisis Strikes

How well you, your company, or your social concern reacts in a crisis determines the success of all communications efforts—crisis and "business as usual" alike.

Maintaining a good public image demands that you have a crisis—or challenge—communications plan in place, and in writing, to help you think on your feet. The cornerstone of the plan is agreeing on how to respond to bad news.

Before formulating your own crisis management plan, observe other organizations in action, including Johnson & Johnson, Morton-Thiokol, and NASA. What follows are mini case histories of Tylenol and *Challenger* to show an example of bad news badly handled, and an example of how skillful management of bad news helped win back consumer confidence and respect.

142

Good public relations people are good because they can quickly identify a silver lining in a cloud of adversity. That's what they are paid to do—to maintain a constructive attitude regardless of the situation. The immediate, intuitive response of a public relations professional in a crisis is to consider a bad situation a challenge rather than a disaster. Johnson & Johnson's quick, positive response to the Tylenol poisonings in Chicago, for example (in which at least seven people died after taking Extra-Strength Tylenol capsules that had been laced with cyanide), helped save the company's dominant market share in headache remedies. By being honest with the public about its role, and by appearing to uphold the corporate sense of social responsibility, the company avoided panic and earned the public's trust. Another result of the scare was the introduction of tamper-resistant packaging.

The United States government, on the other hand, gets low marks for its handling of the aftermath of the *Challenger* tragedy. In addition, the tactic of including a schoolteacher, Christa MacAuliffe, in the crew backfired because her participation made the failure of the rocket launch all the more poignant to the public.

Loss of Challenger/*Loss of Faith*

The January 28, 1986, explosion of the *Challenger* space shuttle on live television is an event most Americans will long remember. It stands right next to the assassination of John F. Kennedy as the kind of shattering experience in which you tend to remember where you were when you first heard the news.

The *Challenger* disaster, in addition to killing six astronauts and a schoolteacher, threatened America's technological prowess and severely hobbled the country's efforts in the space race.

While the nation grieved in disbelief and waited to hear from its leaders, NASA repeatedly postponed its first press conference. When the agency spokesperson finally came on camera, he did not have a sufficient level of authority to be convincing. Even worse, he appeared wooden and unresponsive to questions.

From a logistics standpoint, the press conference was a flop. It was conducted in the shade, with bright sunshine in the background—heightening the sense of being in the shadows, of concealing the facts.

All this contributed to the public's feeling of disbelief and a dismaying awareness that the agency, and the nation's leaders, didn't know what they were doing. Even then-President Reagan, who generally got high marks for good use of public relations, failed to talk to the nation effectively about the tragedy.

The brunt of negative publicity was borne by the company that manufactured the booster rockets and the faulty rocket-motor seal. Charles S. Locke, chairman and CEO of Morton-Thiokol, has said that before the accident "we were unknown in the press." Thus, telling the company's side of the story might not have had a positive effect. Locke also said in an interview with *Business Week* that talking to the press before they understood what had happened would have led to speculation and the eventual feeling that the company had lied if the investigation led to some other conclusions. "Basically," he said in that interview, "we are all frustrated chemists. And we're not terribly PR-minded."

Two years later, Locke remained convinced that speaking out after the crisis would not have been the best policy. "It's just not my nature," he said.

Though Morton-Thiokol received harsh criticism, the company endured the communications crisis to emerge secure in its bottom line. For the most part, costs were covered by insurance. Within two years, the company's stock price was 22 percent higher than before the accident. This worst-case scenario did not concern a consumer product, however. During the aftermath of the *Challenger* disaster, the public's belief in its government and support of the space program did suffer—showing that doing public relations for the space program might be the most complicated assignment in the communications field.

Morton-Thiokol's string of crises continued. Former engineers who said they warned against the launch later said they were punished for doing so. Within months, disclosures revealed the existence of an FBI probe into alleged fraud at the company.

In October 1987, a former Thiokol purchasing agent was among several people indicted in connection with a fraud and kickback scheme that included materials used in shuttle and weapons work. Two months later, a fire killed five Thiokol employees and destroyed part of the plant where the company was building the MX missile.

January 1988 brought more disappointment and poor image-making for Thiokol, when results of tests revealed new design problems and caused NASA to postpone a planned launch. In the spring of 1988, however, Locke was still resisting the need to work with, not against, the press. He was quoted as saying, "I may have become meaner and harder, with a thicker skin." The opportunity for good public relations—like the Bay checkerspot—had fluttered by.

Now the Good News:
Tylenol—Truth and Recall

The 1982 Tylenol tragedy was unique in American history and presented the manufacturer, Johnson & Johnson, with its greatest challenge in its ninety-six years. The crisis communications plan had to address forcefully the following issues:

- Dealing with the crisis
- Cooperating with the press
- Drafting and executing a public relations plan that would bring the brand back from the edge of extinction.

The handling of the Tylenol situation proved to be a benchmark for the public relations profession. From the beginning, public relations people were included in meetings at the highest level to help write policy, measure attitudes, and formulate strategy to bring about a successful comeback for the brand.

Johnson & Johnson introduced Tylenol in 1975 and, through marketing muscle and strong endorsement from the medical profession, by 1982 had captured 37 percent of the $1-billion analgesic market for pain relievers, contributing an estimated 7 percent of the company's worldwide sales and 15 to 20 percent of its 1981 profits. The product had become the brand of choice for 100 million Americans and represented more than the combined dollar sales of the older brands—Anacin, Bayer, Bufferin, and Excedrin.

Though Tylenol held more than 35 percent of the analgesic market before the poisonings, its market share plunged to 13 percent after the deaths were made public. A product designed to help people had been used in what company spokespersons called "an act of terrorism." Many analysts, in fact, said the Tylenol business was destroyed forever.

In just five months, however, Tylenol recaptured 70 percent of the market it once held. How was it done? First, following the poisonings, Johnson & Johnson withdrew all Tylenol capsules nationally and established a $100,000 reward for information.

Immediately after the poisonings were announced, 93,000 bottles of Tylenol capsules were recalled and telegrams sent to doctors, hospitals, and distributors— at a cost of half a million dollars. All advertising was suspended, with the exception of several television spots to reassure the public.

The company then went into the first phase of dealing with the crisis: simply trying to understand what happened. It wasn't easy. All leads ended in a confusing mass of information. Initially, at least 250 other related illnesses and deaths in the nation were believed to be Tylenol-related.

A team consisting of a management representative, a lawyer, a public relations aide, and a security person was assembled to coordinate the company's response. Moreover, a Johnson & Johnson crisis group began meeting twice a day with an executive committee member, group chairman, president, chairman, vice-president of public relations, consumer products chairman, and general counsel.

While the crisis was still at its peak, Johnson & Johnson planned a public relations program that would include every available technique, including attitude sampling research/surveys and video press conferences via satellite. The target audiences included employees, stockholders, medical professionals, every segment of consumer, medical and trade press, legislators, opinion makers, and the public.

During this crisis, the company's relationship with

the press improved. The company needed the media to get the correct information out to the public immediately and to help prevent panic. The cyanide-laced Extra-Strength Tylenol capsules posed a uniquely threatening situation.

When Johnson & Johnson had sufficient proof that the tamperings that poisoned the seven people in Chicago had not taken place during the manufacturing process, it could then proceed to the second phase of recovery—assessing the impact. While the first phase focused on problem identification, this phase emphasized communication. This is the stage where research, another public relations function, comes in.

Johnson & Johnson's major advertising agency, Young & Rubicam, undertook market research. The results indicated that an amazing 94 percent of the consumers surveyed knew that Tylenol had been involved in poisonings—probably more people than those who know who is currently President of the United States.

Of the survey group, though 87 percent knew that the manufacturer was not responsible for the deaths, 61 percent said they were unlikely to buy Tylenol capsules in the future, and 50 percent felt that way about Tylenol tablets, even though only the capsules were involved.

The vital hook on which the recovery strategy was based, however, was that the same surveys indicated frequent Tylenol users seemed more inclined to use the product again. The message, as interpreted by the company? Forget new customers for now, but bring the old ones back into the fold.

Phase Three, therefore, would be the mammoth task of bringing the brand name back to life.

According to company executives, dropping the brand name was never part of their worst-case scenario. Given only half of its previous market share, they reasoned, the brand would still be the market leader.

The comeback started with a national sales meeting in November 1982. Within a few weeks, Tylenol capsules were back on the shelves in triple-sealed, tamper-resistant packages. Johnson & Johnson issued newspaper coupons, worth $2.50, to replace supplies of Tylenol—80 million of them. Consumers could also call a toll-free number for coupons—430,000 calls were received. This coupon strategy was later credited as having the most positive effect on saving the brand.

For a public relations practitioner, these would be heady times. Johnson & Johnson could not escape the attention of the press. An estimated 125,000 articles (estimated by a New York University marketing professor as being worth $100 million for that level of advertising) covered the poisonings and the aftermath. In addition, for internal morale, Johnson & Johnson's public relations department assembled a one-hour videotape of news reports on the Tylenol tragedy, including comments by company officials. The tape was shown on the company's employee television network.

The company also sent about two million pieces of literature to doctors, dentists, nurses, and pharmacists, reminding them that Johnson & Johnson was not responsible for the deaths. The messages asked for them to reassure patients that Tylenol products were not at risk. The sales force, augmented by other company divisions, personally took the message to distributors and important customers.

Satellite conferencing reached 600 reporters in 30 cities. Competing with the death of Russian leader Leonid Brezhnev, the Tylenol comeback was the second leading story of the day.

Several management representatives appeared on major television shows, including "Nightline," "Today," "The Phil Donohue Show," and "60 Minutes." Other television appearances by management were shown in more than fifty locations.

Comments were covered by print, television, and radio. The company's log of all media requests records more than 2,500, many requiring follow-up information.

In 1986, when a Peekskill, New York, woman died after taking Extra-Strength Tylenol capsules, Johnson & Johnson recalled, and terminated the manufacture and sale of, nonprescription capsules. The company estimated that the free consumer exchange for other forms of the product, offered in 1986, was $150 million in pretax charges against first-quarter earnings. Moreover, the cost of the product recall and rebuilding of market share was expected to be $100 to $150 million after taxes for the year. But the public image of Johnson & Johnson remains untarnished, and Tylenol caplets continue to sell well.

9

Coping with Bad Press: Taking the Bitter with the Sweet

You may think of yourself or your organization as crisis-proof, but just consider Three Mile Island, the Pinto and Corvair, Rely tampons, Love Canal, the Dalkon Shield, Union Carbide in Bhopal, the Hyatt Regency skywalks, earthquakes in Mexico, floods in Colombia, and a possible Elvis Presley sighting in your employee cafeteria.

As for possible issues, you have only to contemplate: fires, explosions, and bombed theaters; OSHA violations and lawsuits; strikes, layoffs, and poor earnings; product defects and product tamperings; proxy fights, takeovers, and mergers; nuclear power; right-to-life; conservation; minority and women's rights; white-collar crime; and terrorism.

And you don't know how long you'll need to worry about those issues. For example, Love Canal came back

153

to haunt Hooker Chemical *twenty-five years* after the company turned the area into a chemical dump site.

The critical question is, When is it a crisis?

You have a crisis when:

- A situation involves death or serious injury requiring hospitalization
- Any violent or nonviolent action from individuals or groups prevents the normal functioning of a business or organization
- A situation attracts regional or national news media to your place of business or organization

If you are still not convinced that your group needs a crisis communications plan, consider the Suzuki Samurai—a utility sports vehicle with so many problems associated with "rollover" that comic Jay Leno has gained a reputation for his routine of Samurai jokes. (Example: Have you seen the upside-down eye chart that's part of the driver's test for Samurai drivers?)

When Suzuki learned that *Consumer Reports* was about to seriously criticize the vehicle in an upcoming issue and in effect ask for its recall, Suzuki management decided the best offense is a good defense. By buying up all prime-time television time available to them, they attempted to gain equal access, even if they had to pay for it. In the ten days following a *Consumer Reports* press conference covering the issue of Suzuki Samurai rollover, Suzuki spent $1.5 million over and above its normal advertising budget to air ads quoting positive reviews.

Suzuki also bought satellite time to transmit a video press release for use as background material by local television stations. This would be considered a proactive, rather than reactive, public relations technique. (To be proactive, you plan ahead. Reactive measures are done in response to, or after, a crisis. They tend not to be as planned as proactive responses.) To communicate with internal audiences, each dealer received a videotape of the Suzuki press conference and press materials. Suzuki also set up a toll-free number for customers to call with questions.

Setting Up Standby Measures

Appoint a Spokesperson

In public relations planning, your group, whatever your purpose or size, should follow the examples of some Fortune 500 companies in their attempts to "speak with one voice" in times of crisis and media attention. In many of these corporations, a high-level person, and at least one alternate, is chosen as corporate spokesperson. Everyone in the company is requested to deal with the press only through this spokesperson.

By using a designated spokesperson, you help ensure accuracy, consistency, and sensitivity to corporate or organizational concerns when you are represented in the media. The designated spokesperson should:

- Have an extensive and complete knowledge of the business or organization.
- Be as good a listener as speaker.
- Appear assertive but not aggressive.
- Represent the ability to make decisions, meet deadlines, and honor promises.
- Come across as straightforward and honest.

Set Up a Crisis Communications Team

No crisis communications manager is an island. The crisis communications plan that you develop should result from group effort and cooperation.

Each department in your organization will have different concerns. For example, the human resources staff might be sensitive to employment practices, while the company comptroller or organization treasurer might see the financial picture as a potential cause for bad press. In a creative brainstorming session, each representative should be able to construct a "worst-case" scenario to make everyone aware of potentially damaging areas of concern, as well as the best, most consistent ways to handle the situation.

We recommend that you recruit a team from these possible areas of support:

- Public relations
- Management
- Human resources
- Safety/security
- Legal
- Facilities
- Production/manufacturing
- Investor/stockholder relations
- Marketing/advertising/telemarketing
- Data processing/office services

Helpful questions to ask are: What are the greatest risks? How severe would the impact be? What groups would be affected? Vulnerabilities exist at every level of a company or organization. You also have various audiences to consider. For example, while Love Canal got lots of national attention, the public relations person who was on the scene says that the residents of that Niagara Falls neighborhood were the most important public audience to consider, followed by company shareholders, the chemical industry, customers and suppliers of Hooker Chemical, the financial community, government officials, and the public at large.

Involve Top Management and Local Officials

CEOs and organization heads should be willing to commit the human and financial resources needed to develop and maintain a crisis communications plan. Without support from the top, any effort to establish and use such a plan will remain in the planning stage. In a recent survey conducted by a large public relations firm, about half of medium to large U.S. corporations said they had a crisis communications plan in place. Some groups and organizations are more likely to have one than others.

Financial institutions, electrical utilities, and the extractive industries, including mining and gas exploration, as well as nonprofits that serve critical human needs, are most alert to the risks that any business entails when it arouses negative publicity. And in the wake of Three Mile Island, it is now obligatory that nuclear power companies have a crisis communications plan in place—one that has been renewed and approved by corporate management.

Everyone should know what everyone else will do in an emergency. If you represent a manufacturing company, inform the local fire and police departments of your strategies for handling on-site problems.

For the step-by-steps on writing a plan, whether crisis communications or others, see Chapter 2.

Your Role as a Public Relations Professional

You as the public relations professional prepare the press release that announces a crisis or disaster and arrange for any press conference required. You also are

the probable spokesperson. Emergency press headquarters can be set up in a hotel or motel near the
scene. You will need to arrange for telephones, portable
computers, food and coffee, and transportation and
escort services.

In preparing releases, be certain that all information
is accurate and doesn't compromise the company or
organization. To avoid being misquoted, follow up all
oral interviews with a press release giving the facts.
Experienced public relations practitioners recommend
that you correct wrong or misleading information immediately, before it becomes part of the public record.

The media will want to know:

1. *What happened?* What product(s) were involved,
and what are their characteristics? The nature of the
accident; injury to staff, employees, general public;
damage to property and equipment; repairs needed;
length of time required to bring the crisis under control. It is helpful—if not required—to have on hand a
background article for every process your company
represents.

2. *Who is involved?* The nature and extent of injuries
with names, ages, addresses, job titles; what the injured
were doing at the scene; where they were taken. This
information is released only *after families are notified.*
The media expects you to observe this rule.

3. *When?* Day, date, and time of incident.

4. *Where?* The exact location, and the approximate
distance from urban area, local landmark, highway, etc.

5. *Why?* The cause, if known. Do not speculate or go "off the record." Give the current situation only as it can be verified by established information. Also, give the status of the investigation and who is investigating—which government agencies are notified and/or on the scene. (Your job may also include notifying authorities that there is a crisis or accident.)

They Don't Shoot the Messenger, Do They?

If you are the spokesperson for your company or organization during a crisis or emergency, these suggestions will be helpful.

- Emphasize the positive. Be quick to highlight long safety records and acts of heroism on the part of employees or rescuers.
- Tell the truth. Think of Winston Churchill's 1940 radio speech, when he began, "The news from France is very bad."
- Never refuse information. If you don't have the facts, give a good reason why they are not yet available or why you can't disclose them yet.
- Take the names and telephone numbers of reporters when they ask you for information you don't yet have, and tell them you'll get back to them when you do have all the information. Then do for them exactly

what you said you would—call as soon as you can with the information you promised. Prompt, courteous follow-up is essential to maintaining good relations with media representatives.

- Build confidence by appearing concerned but never worried. Display and encourage a positive attitude.
- Don't let a vacuum develop. Be quick with the facts. Otherwise, other, less favorable opinions may dominate the news coverage of your company or event.
- Don't cover up facts or exaggerate the trouble.
- Don't guess at the cause of any accident.
- Never give an answer you're not sure will stand up.
- Have experts ready to speak on your company's or organization's behalf.
- Have press materials on hand, each kit suited for an appropriate situation, in your "suitcase newsroom." One big chemical company has traveling press kits designed for each product or technology it represents, mobile press centers, and a railroad press car to handle large-scale crises.
- Communicate every step of the way throughout the company or organization. (Here is where a crisis communications plan is indispensable, indicating who in the organization or corporate structure receives and transmits news.) An accident at one company location, for example, will trigger the media's interest wherever else you are doing business. All location managers should be prepared.

Follow-up: Designing a Program to Recoup Your Good Name

Disasters come large and small, short term, and long lasting. But sooner or later the immediate crisis ends, and it is your job to restore continuity and trust with all concerned. You will want to direct reassurances to company employees and organizational staff, customers and clients, suppliers and visitors, families, neighbors and the general community, government agencies, stockholders, and market analysts, among others.

First, hold a meeting of the emergency communications team to assess how well the plan operated and note suggestions for improvements. Arrange for the collection of copies of all stories, videotapes, or transcripts of broadcast news.

Then, prepare a concise, candid summary assessing how the emergency communications plan operated, making any recommendations for improvements or modifications. The final follow-up report to your various publics might take the form of a reassuring letter, mailgram, Telex, newsletter, telephone call, personal visit, or even satellite transmission—or a combination.

10

Significant Others: Working Effectively with Supporting Players

Whether you choose a career in public relations as a whole or are interested in only one aspect of the field, such as publicity, the tasks you perform—and, more important, the level of competence you achieve—will often depend on your ability to work with other professionals in the industry.

Your ability as a public relations practitioner to communicate effectively requires a working knowledge of the skills and terminology of the typesetter, photographer, stylist, retoucher, graphic designer, mechanical artist, printer, paper company rep, caterer, events planners, audiovisual equipment technician, celebrity agent, contest creator, trade show organizer, direct-mail fulfillment house, instant printer, computer people, and editorial people—to name but a few!

Working with Photographers

You need to understand something about creative people and what it takes to motivate them when you hire a photographer. Photographers can be described as anything from prima donna to down to earth, from wildly creative to pedestrian. But good photography enhances most communications work, so it's worthwhile to get along with all styles and moods of photographers.

Different communications goals require different approaches. The person who photographs landscapes to Ansel Adams-like perfection for the annual report might not be able to deliver a good 8 by 10-inch black-and-white product shot for a press kit. Some photographers are excellent at capturing actual news events, while others prefer the studio environment. Photographs of everything from a company picnic to company product, corporate staff to volunteers at a non-profit organization, to accidents and other crisis situations require a unique approach tailored to that particular event. Your job is to match the photographer with the situation and the budget.

Ask art directors and printers about photographers they enjoy working with. Look through the Yellow Pages. And the local newspaper often has a photographer on staff who will accept freelance assignments. This choice is appropriate because most public relations photography is photojournalistic in intent. As you're interviewing photographers, ask to see their portfolios.

The Professional Society of Magazine Photographers (ASMP) makes recommendations from among its 5,000 members. The national headquarters is 419 Park Avenue South, New York, NY 10016, (212) 889-9144.

Some perfectly conventional photography is required to cover your bases by having on file 8 by 10-inch black-and-white head-and-shoulders photographs of your key management people. As you develop communications tools—articles, releases, fact sheets, and backgrounders—you'll find the best placement opportunities often demand great still photography and sometimes videotape.

Even if you produce your own photography, you will still find yourself in situations where you have to hire a photographer. Be sure you determine:

- Usage and contract. Get this in writing. A photo for a newsletter will be much less expensive than one for a national advertisement.
- The half- or full-day rate ($1,500 per day plus expenses and prints is average). By being organized and knowing exactly what you want, you can save time and money.
- Who pays for materials (prints, film, props, stylist)?
- Who provides models, and at what cost?
- Who holds the copyrights for all uses of the photography? Be sure you own what you are paying for.
- Will you attend the photo session? Ask for a Polaroid "check print" to double check the details *before* you approve the final composition.

To get the best performance with each photographer, reward creativity and extra hard work. Photographers, who in a way make something out of nothing, usually think of themselves as artists and take great pride in their work. Try to not hurt their feelings. Some are fierce. Let them know if you would like their suggestions or else make it clear that yours is the only vision they need to understand.

Some photographers may scorn public relations budgets, which are considerably tighter than those of the Rich Big Sister—advertising. But most photographers need more work.

How Public Relations Uses Photography

In public relations, photographs are often used to support or expand the viewer's understanding of what the article or caption is about. Rarely does an 8 × 10-inch glossy of two business executives shaking hands with each other (called a "grip and grin") do an adequate job. The photograph must be technically correct. Black-and-white photography is still preferable for print media. Television stations, however, like to look at color slides to get some understanding of the event, even if they ultimately don't use the photographs.

People love photographs of important events. Good public relations often means doing the right thing at the right time. You therefore may want to include professional-quality photography, suitable for framing, in follow-up letters, particularly if you are fund-raising or looking for a vote of confidence. Remember that special events frequently have budgets that allow for extras. Why not enhance the public relations opportunities by having attention-getting photography of the event on hand?

The image should have impact, meaning, and fresh, sharp composition and should be in a format to fulfill the assignment. Magazine covers, for example, are almost always strong vertical photographs with space at the top for the type or logo. If you have a chance to provide the cover shot, make sure the photograph fits the format. A horizontal image in this instance will not work.

Slide shows are all one way—either vertical or horizontal. It's true that either format can be "masked" by hand to fit, but this distracts from the visual image and adds significantly to costs.

Working with Graphic Artists, Typesetters, Printers, and Others

The best way to understand what graphic artists, typesetters, and printers do is to visit a printing company of any size. Call the company and ask for a sales representative to take you on a tour. The company will invest the time with you because the visit could lead to new business. Many printing companies have in-house

PROOFREADERS' MARKS

OPERATIONAL SIGNS

ℐ	Delete
⌒	Close up; delete space
ℬ	Delete and close up
#	Insert space
eq #	Make space between words equal; make leading between lines equal
hr #	Insert hair space
ls	Letterspace
¶	Begin new paragraph
no ¶	Run paragraphs together
☐	Move type one em from left or right
]	Move right
[	Move left
][	Center
⊓	Move up
⊔	Move down
=	Straighten type; align horizontally
‖	Align vertically
tr	Transpose
sp	Spell out
stet	Let it stand
⊥	Push down type; check type image

TYPOGRAPHICAL SIGNS

lc	Lowercase capital letter
cap	Capitalize lowercase letter
sc	Set in small capitals
ital	Set in italic type
rom	Set in roman type
bf	Set in boldface type
wf	Wrong font; set in correct type
x	Reset broken letter; check repro or film
⤾	Reverse (type upside down)

PUNCTUATION MARKS

⌃	Insert comma
⌄	Insert apostrophe (or single quotation mark)
⌄⌄	Insert quotation marks
⊙	Insert period
?	Insert question mark
;/	Insert semicolon
:/	Insert colon
|=|	Insert hyphen
⅟	Insert em dash
⅟	Insert en dash

graphic artists and in-house typesetters. Have questions ready to ask throughout the tour.

Graphic artists are the starting point in producing a well-designed and attractive printed piece, from a sign to indicate a designated parking spot to a corporate or organizational annual report. They also perform other graphics assignments, such as creating storyboards used in television and videotape, and designing models, technical aids, and multimedia works.

Aside from the basic requirement of project design, the graphic artist or designer will also help you pin down and resolve the countless, essential details of the project. Paper size and stock; reproduction method (including color, overlays, versions); printing process; folding and shipping; and approvals are just a few examples. You must determine the purpose and requirements of an assignment before the graphic artist or designer can give a useful cost estimate.

The graphic artist or designer will usually be able to supervise the production of an assignment, from initial concept to finished piece, if this is a function you don't plan to perform. It is also routine for many art directors or designers to hire outside talent for illustration and photography. Be sure the project budget and deadlines can support this.

If you are shopping for a graphic artist or designer, call a professional organization or look in the Yellow Pages. Often an artist's representative, rather than the artist, will show you a portfolio of completed assignments. If you have a strong creative approach of your own in mind, share ads, campaigns, photographs, and artwork to focus and spark the communication.

If you have the opportunity, work with a graphic designer to construct a "comp"—a rough sketch of what the final photograph or illustration should look like. An organizational or corporate symbol, called the "logo," in the background provides a gentle reminder of who paid for the print. However, readily identifiable logos also make your photographs more commercial than newsworthy.

The graphic designer may also use or recommend a particular typesetter. Printers often have in-house capabilities. Or, you may choose a desktop publishing system that approximates typesetting capabilities. Whoever prepares your copy to be typeset, be sure that the details of typesetting—type size, type style, letter fit, line spacing, and hyphenation—are determined *before* work is begun.

Editorial Support

You want the finished product to be well written, polished, and error-free. The more familiar you are with a text, the less likely you are to spot even simple errors. It is always a good idea to have a copyeditor review your work before it goes into production, and a proofreader to check it during production. Copyeditors and proofreaders are paid because they are good at correcting

Helvetica	Helvetica Cond.	Times Roman
6 Mandi	6 Mandi	6 Mandi
7 Mandi	7 Mandi	7 Mandi
8 Mandi	8 Mandi	8 Mandi
9 Mandi	9 Mandi	9 Mandi
10 Mandi	10 Mandi	10 Mandi
11 Mandi	11 Mandi	11 Mandi
12 Mandi	12 Mandi	12 Mandi
14 Mandi	14 Mandi	14 Mandi
16 Mandi	16 Mandi	16 Mandi
18 Mandi	18 Mandi	18 Mandi
20 Mandi	20 Mandi	20 Mandi
24 Mandi	24 Mandi	24 Mandi
30 Mandi	30 Mandi	30 Mandi
36 Manc	36 Mand	36 Mand
48 Mar	48 Mar	48 Man
60 Ma	60 Ma	60 Ma
72 Ma	72 Ma	72 Ma
84 M	84 M	84 M

other people's grammar, wording, spelling, punctuation, and syntax. In order to benefit from the knowledge and expertise they have to share, keep a copy of essential proofreading marks—the shorthand that helps eliminate mistakes.

The Mechanical Artist

Once a document is typeset, proofread, and approved, a mechanical artist, sometimes called a board artist, arranges the type (called "repros") and any original art or photography on a board according to the layout. The finished board is called a "mech," or mechanical. When finished, it is then "camera ready," which means it is ready for the printer for reproduction. (In desktop publishing, this step is done on the computer.)

Factors that need to be determined in the mechanical stage are size, color, paper stock, reproduction method, binding and folding, color correction, color separation, use of transfer type, photostats, art, tone indication, hand lettering, scaling, retouching, cropping, and overlays, as well as delivery date, design, shipping, legal or approval cycles, and—of course—adherence to budget.

The Retoucher: Picking Up Where Nature Left Off

Did you ever wonder why movie stars continue to look so good even as they age? The artist is not only the makeup person but also the retoucher. A retoucher can manually and mechanically correct contrast, remove flaws, change mood, and add detail and focus to a photograph.

One of the top executives in the Gannett Rochester Newspapers once had a portrait completely retouched to make him appear to be looking to the left when it was taken looking to the right. Apparently he didn't want to have his photo redone. So the retoucher, a true artist, carefully reversed his hair part, buttons, and rings.

The Printer: The Transformer

The printer is the magician who transforms the mechanical into a finished product. This includes processes that range from basic offset, die cutting, and embossing to four-color work and three-D imaging.

Usually the art director or production person is the direct line to the printer, but it is often part of the public relations function: You, in other words, will be the liaison. What the printer will want to know about each job is: size, color, stock, color specifications, contrast, binding, folding, ink, approvals, budget, delivery, type of reproduction proofs required, use, and number of plates needed. It helps if you provide a layout, even a rough layout, when you send the job to the printer.

Afterword

This book began with a butterfly story that showed how having the right attitude saved one company from a bad image. The media is full of other examples of people who heard opportunity knocking, and of those who ignored it.

Once you read this book, you may understand why the citizens of Owenton, Kentucky, stretched a huge white banner over Main Street with the message: "Owen County needs a doctor. Inquire at Courthouse." The community brought nationwide media attention to their plight—which is anything but unique in small-town America—as well as some much-needed job applicants.

Or you might appreciate what led the citizens of West Cape May, New Jersey, to inaugurate a Lima Bean Association and Festival. In addition to some light-hearted boosterism, the Preservation Society of the

Lima Bean sought to call attention to South Jersey's vanishing farmlands, noted for their lima bean farms. "Fewer mini-malls and more limas" served as a rallying cry as first-graders made lima bean soup and more than fifty contestants vied to be Miss Lima Bean.

Ten thousand people enjoyed the lima bean festival, while conservationists relied on the lowly bean for grass-roots support—and got it. The media loved the event, and the effort to save the farmlands was established in a nonthreatening manner.

We hope you are equally successful in your public relations efforts, and that you enjoy the process of creating good public relations programs and materials as much as we have throughout our own careers.

Glossary of Print Production Terms

Bleed (or full bleed): The extension of the printed image to the edge of the sheet or page.

Comping: A mathematical formula used to determine how much copy will fit in a given space, based on type size, style, leading, and page-size requirements.

Dummy: A final layout that shows the position of illustrations and text as they will appear in the final reproduction, cut to the size and shape of the finished piece.

Duotone: A two-color halftone reproduction made from a one-color photograph.

Galley (or galley proof): Columnar version of the typeset copy, given to the client for review and proofreading but not yet positioned according to layout.

Halftone: The reproduction of continuous-tone artwork, such as a photograph, through a crossline or contact screen that converts the image into dots of various sizes.

Hickey: A spot or imperfection in the printing due to such things as dirt on the press, dried ink skin, or paper particles. A hickey often looks like a tiny white circle.

Layout: The drawing or sketch of a proposed printed piece, showing areas for both type and illustrations.

Leading: The amount of space between two lines of type, usually measured from baseline to baseline of type.

Mechanical: The camera-ready pasteup of type and artwork on a board. Includes all type, photos (indicated only), and line art. The mechanical is marked for any color breaks in printing.

Pica: Printer's unit of measure, used for measuring line length and copy depth. There are 12 points in a pica and 6 picas in an inch.

Point: Printer's unit of measure, used for designating type sizes. There are approximately 72 points in an inch.

Press proof (goes by many names, including brownline or blueline): A proof of a color subject made in advance of the production run. The proof is the last production stage presented to the client for review and signoff before the beginning of the actual printing.

Screen: In color printing, the method used to reproduce color gradations.

Stat (or photostat): A black-and-white image on photographic paper that can be used for reproduction. Reproductions will be in black and white only and will show only what is on the stat. Stats can be reduced or enlarged.

Thumbnail sketch: A small drawing of what a finished page might look like; an extremely rough version, usually used early in the design process.

Type size: Sizes range from 5 to 72 point. Text type is 14 point and smaller; display type is larger than 14 point.

Widow: A single word or several words at the end of a paragraph that appears on a line by itself at the top of a page. Less than two lines of type at the top of a page is not desirable in good typesetting.

Adapted from *Pocket Pal: A Graphic Arts Production Handbook,* by Michael Bruno. International Paper Company, 220 East 42nd Street, New York, NY 10017.

Index

See also Glossary, p. 177–179